Releasing Your Pet's Hidden Health Potential

DR. RICHARD PALMQUIST

Forward by Cornelia Guest

The author has made every effort to provide timely and accurate information in the preparation of this text. The reader should recognize that scientific and clinical knowledge and application are constantly evolving, and since proper treatment requires consideration of the individual patient circumstances, nothing in this text should be taken as a proper protocol for any specific disease entity. Veterinary care should be properly delivered by a licensed and qualified veterinarian with proper client education and consent. This text is not a substitute for proper professional education and a doctor-patient relationship and use in any way other than as a learning text could lead to nonoptimal outcomes. No guarantee or liability is accepted by the author or publisher for results obtained from use of this material.

ISBN: 1449908446
ISBN-13: 9781449908447

The riddles of health and disease truly have simple answers. Unfortunately, the fields of science and medicine have turned the power of simplicity into a turbulence of complexity, thus losing basic tenets of healing. Dr. Palmquist has gotten in touch with the core of natural healing and shares many of its aspects in this wonderful book.

—**Marty Goldstein, DVM,** Director of the Smith Ridge Veterinary Center, Ask Martha's Vet national radio talk show host, and author of The Nature of Animal Healing.

My journey to embrace holistic, complementary medicine began in the mid-1970s when I was studying the potential of vaccinations to precipitate adverse events in companion animals. Now, after nearly fifty years as a clinician/scientist in veterinary medicine, my true focus is solidly on holism and the power of healing. Rick Palmquist is a colleague much to be admired, for his quest is both selfless and compassionate. He strives to learn, share, and apply his knowledge and experience to benefit his patients and their caregivers, not only to heal but also to lift their spirits. Continue to blaze your trail, my dear friend!

—**Jean Dodds, DVM**, Founder of Hemopet, vaccine reformer, holistic clinician, researcher, and international speaker in integrative medicine.

We are occasionally gifted in life with knowing people who share our vision of what life should and could be. Some of those people have immense insight into discernment of truth, and translation of that which they have studied, into useful data. Rick is truly one of those rare individuals whose passion for what is right and whose thirst for knowledge have led him down the path of enlightened healing. He is ever in search of biological therapeutics, and his continual quest for unearthing the very <u>best</u> methods for improving the status of patients entrusted to his care have brought him a wealth of information in many disciplines of medicine. He brings his huge personality and quirky sense of humor into every relationship he builds, whether it is with a human or an animal.

Mr. Webster defines the word "heal" thus: "to make sound or whole, to restore to health, to cause an undesirable condition to be overcome, to restore to original purity or integrity." In every sense of the word, Dr. Palmquist embodies the meaning of "healer." My sincere hope is that you find yourself captivated by this book, and learn what he is so willing to share.

—**Paula Jo Broadfoot, DVM**, Broadfoot Veterinary Clinic, Van Buren, Arkansas, AHVMA board of directors, veterinary homotoxicology consultant, author, and national speaker in alternative medicine.

I have been honored to collaborate with Dr. Rick Palmquist on hundreds of cases over the last decade. He is the perfect balance of science, intuition, and poetry, a synthesis that brings the practice of medicine to the level of high art. Art in its highest form bringing to light the inner truth producing an alchemy that's outcome is both tangible and other-dimensional healing. His brilliance of mind and generosity of spirit is shared with equal passion whether he works with a private client referral or one of my rescue animals that has only a meager budget for medical assistance. For the privilege to work, laugh and cry beside Dr. Rick on this journey of healing the bodies, hearts, and souls of The Animals, I thank Divine Intelligence.

—**Janet M. Hicks**, Animal Communicator/Healer, CEO The Bumper Foundation, a 501c3 Rescue for Animals.

Dr. Palmquist brilliantly integrates spirituality and veterinary science in a way that is refreshing as well as comfortable for the reader. This book makes good sense for those who live with and care for animals to follow its wisdom.

—**Robert S. Goldstein VMD**, Director of Veterinary Services for Healing Center for Animals and Animal Nutrition Technologies in Westport, Connecticut. Editor and Coauthor, Integrating Complementary Medicine into Veterinary Practice and Coauthor with Susan J Goldstein of The Goldstein Guide To Wellness and Longevity.

Disclaimer:

This book was published with the intent to provide readers with accurate and authoritative information in regard to the subject matter within. While every precaution has been taken in preparation of this book, the author and publisher expressly disclaim any responsibility for any errors, omissions, or adverse effects arising from use or application of the material presented herein. The techniques and suggestions are used at the reader's discretion and are not to be construed as a substitute for veterinary care from a competent veterinarian who is properly trained in the use of these modalities. If you suspect a medical problem you should consult your veterinarian for specific advice. Professionals should not consider this text as a complete training manual and should seek proper professional training and certification before performing these procedures. Muscle response testing is not a diagnostic procedure and is only useful in assisting with selecting agents that may be helpful to the body's natural healing efforts. In no case should muscle response testing be used as a primary diagnostic modality.

✫ ✫ ✫

Acknowledgements

My life is a constant journey to find usable truth. In that journey many heaven-sent beings have assisted me. My parents provided me with a rich experience and set examples that were hard for me to live up to, while my animal friends introduced me to science, absorbed my tears, shared my laughter, and made life a pleasant experience. My college professional advisor, Ed Richards, set my feet firmly on the path to veterinary professional school; the faculty at Colorado State University, particularly David Twedt and Mike Leib, who demonstrated unswerving dedication to healing, made me aspire to greater heights. My first professional employer, Weston Richter, taught me about getting many things done while never compromising medical quality. Marty Goldstein introduced me to alternative medicine and converted me from skeptic to practitioner. In large part I owe my success in alternative medicine to my friend and mentor, PJ Broadfoot, who took a year of her life to start me on the journey to biological therapy with nutrition and homotoxicology.

In all this work, the world owes those people who established and continue to advance the field of alternative medicine, people such as Carvel Tiekert, who took the American Holistic Veterinary Medical Association (AHVMA) from a dream to a real, working organization dedicated to the advancement of alternative veterinary medicine. The elders, board members, and committee members of

AHVMA all participated in some way in the creation of this work and I owe them much. Likewise, without the amazing organization of muscle testing experience into the Nutrition Response Testing^{SM} protocol taught by Freddie Ulan, I would not be able to do this work at all.

Tracy Petersen helped me once again with editing and Heather Scholl brought the lovely cover art image to life. I am in their debt for their valuable help.

Finally, I need to thank my wife, MJ Brandt, for her constant patience and love; my family for the time they gave me to do the work; and my staff, clients, and patients, without whom none of this work is possible. Joseph Makkar, my hospital operations officer and spiritual brother, provided ethical feedback through his long association in our office. At each juncture of my life a new angel appeared to help me with the next step. Many of these people and animals don't know the extent to which they influenced or helped me. I hope that this book is in some way a tangible expression of my gratitude.

Richard Palmquist, DVM
11.11.09

Foreward

It is said that animals don't talk, don't communicate on our level. As far as I'm concerned they talk and communicate really well. You just have to pay attention... and Dr. Palmquist does just that. He speaks animal. Dog, cat, hamster, lizard; you name it, he speaks it. He is a great communicator, and to be a great healer, you must be a great communicator.

I will never forget meeting Dr. Palmquist for the first time. Bear, my Great Pyrenees, was suffering terribly from allergies. Covered in hotspots he was a miserable, itchy, nervous wreck. I had adopted him a week prior to our visit and I realized once we got to the clinic he thought he was going to be given away yet again. Shaking and cowering in the corner of the room I was heartbroken to see such a lovely, beautiful creature so terrorized. Well, in walked Dr. Palmquist and it all changed! Within seconds he assessed the situation and was on the floor eye to eye with Bear talking, petting, and playing with him. It was a magical transformation. Bear's tail was wagging and he gave Dr. Palmquist his paw; he was alive. Mind you this was the first time I had seen his tail wag. It was love on both our parts for Dr. Palmquist! I knew then that I had found an incredibly gifted healer. Having been raised with animals all my life I knew that Dr. Palmquist was a very special creature. I knew I was in the right place and more importantly so did Bear. That day Dr. Palmquist spent time playing with Bear, observing him, getting to know him, and understanding him, his emotions, and the path he was on. Our journey together had begun and at times it got a bit rocky! Bear's trust in Dr. Palmquist was immediate as was mine. The vast knowledge he has is incredible. Different therapies, different ways to heal all came into play. We would seem to hit a roadblock, and Dr. Palmquist would find another way to heal and within months Bear looked and felt like a different dog. I still don't know who was happier, Bear or Dr. Palmquist. They are both amazing.

Going to the doctor is never fun for anyone...two or four legged! But when you walk into Dr. Palmquist's clinic there is no fear. Everyone is lovely and the animals know they are in the right place—where a lovely man will listen, understand, and take care of their every need in the most loving way possible. It is my wish that every animal on the planet be touched by Dr. Palmquist and with this book my dream will come true.

His incredible compassion and love for what he does is mesmerizing. Through this book we are with him every step of the way—in his exam rooms, learning how he deals with each patient on a very personnel level. I feel so blessed to be a part of his world and to learn from him and share his incredible journey. I know that everyone reading this book will feel the same way. Dr Palmquist, you truly make the world a better place!

Cornelia Guest
November 2009

Dedication

For Yoda

I look upon your face,
And I smile.
I touch your sides,
And I smile.
I feel your ageless warmth,
And I smile.
I think of you,
And I smile.
Yellow core of light,
Smiling at us all,
Brings understanding,
Love, and serenity;
Sourced of Truth,
And so,
We smile.
You are teacher.
You are friend.
Reminder of Divinity,
In all things.
Complete.
Timeless.
Existence perfected.
I touch a tear,
Streaming on my cheek,
And sadness departs.
Because I know you,
I smile.

Table of Contents

Part 1. The Basics of Health

Part 2. Disease and Healing

CHAPTER 8.
Rejuvenation Therapy: Stem Cells **103**

CHAPTER 9.
Vaccinations **109**

CHAPTER 10.
Working with Health Care Professionals **115**

✧ ✧ ✧

Introduction

The Truth about Health

What would you say if I were to tell you that every living thing has some degree of knowledge about survival? Would you nod your head in agreement at the basic common sense of that statement? Or would you reach for a book that proves that life is an accident and that all living things survive because of some cosmic oddity?

Fortunately, it doesn't matter one bit, because this book is about knowledge that can be used and experienced directly by anyone, regardless of his or her religious faith or belief paradigm. This book is about truth and healing. When we seek truth we find healing. When we find healing we find truth. Truth simply "is." No amount of alteration can change it from its basic essence.

Seeking truth and using it to improve health is one of the highest callings. In our office we call this results-oriented medicine (ROM). It is certainly something worth pursuing and it provides me with an interesting life.

I was raised in a very scientific and spiritual household. My parents frequently discussed the wonderful way that life's elements fit together and lead toward higher levels of survival. In this biological world, my parents saw the perfection and handiwork of the Divine, as well as the built-in wisdom of biological systems. My father used to voice his dissatisfaction with people who fought over words without actually just looking and witnessing directly the marvelous world that surrounds us. My mother was brilliant and believed that one secured survival by mastery of books and practice. And so in these two people I had tough taskmasters, but also parents whose love always provided me with a safe space for retreat, honest inquiry, and consideration.

Life fascinates me. From my earliest memories I spent my time looking at things and trying to discern patterns and relationships in this game we call Life. I capitalize this word because I believe that Life is more than just random chemical processes.

As a child I readily saw the truth of the world as a grand place filled with miracles. It was clear and obvious: I have always been surrounded by amazing beings. Living in the company of special people and animals, it's been easy to see Life's greater face. I owe all of these people and animals a tremendous debt for their loving natures, which always serve as trail markers to assist me in finding my way in the world. Much of what is good in me now is there because of their examples.

Animals and Actions

From the time of my earliest memory until now I have been fascinated by animals and living things. My boyhood home was filled with spiders, hermit crabs, fish, frogs, tadpoles, crayfish, crabs, snakes, birds, rabbits, ducks, chickens, geese, cats, and dogs. Animals fed and clothed me. They absorbed my tears, protected me, and shared the joy of my life. It seems to me that animals are naturally rooted in Life. Steeped in the sauce of survival and in loving them, it was only natural that I spent my time pursuing better ways to heal them. In that journey they helped me find myself and the beauty that lies in every vital being I meet.

Working with animals pushed my mind to reach past words and into actual actions and concepts. As humans we depend on words, but they are merely symbols of things and not things themselves. Animals are not impressed by words. They focus upon actions and intentions. Animals seem to have a kindred sense regarding things that benefit their survival. They are the ultimate in results-oriented medicine. We see this every day in our practice—a biting dog relaxes when given the correct treatment program and doesn't care what religion the practitioner might espouse. A fearful, vicious, scratching cat purrs and licks your hand when it realizes that you are there for it and that your treatment isn't going to make it worse. Admittedly, these changes take time, but they usually appear eventually.

For years I fought with cats and struggled with dogs as I tried to force the latest, greatest drug or surgery upon their constitutions. Don't misunderstand me; I still do these things when they are needed. If sedation will calm a cat so I can remove its infected tooth and save its kidneys from further damage, then I happily sedate the cat even if it isn't happy about the procedure. In the past I've saved pets hit by cars, cut by knives, shot by bullets, and suffering from life-threatening infections. Drugs and surgery were and are critical parts of those treatment plans. Using the tools of conventional medicine, I have helped animals live longer, but so often I have found myself frustrated and at a loss in helping many of my patients, especially those with chronic diseases such as arthritis, heart disease, skin problems, and cancer. Professional lectures and texts taught me that the majority of my patients will die of these chronic issues and that there is no cure for them. These texts taught me that many of these conditions are genetic, and that is not something we can address further. They instructed me that our best hope is to suppress the pet's symptoms and keep them alive for a while longer. And so I did that for several years.

But I knew there had to be more to healing than what I had learned in school. After more than two decades of clinical practice and two hundred thousand patient visits, I am pleased to say that there is much more to veterinary medicine than what we teach our students in veterinary schools. And some of the most important things I have learned are not in textbooks or professional school lectures. Some of the most powerful healing secrets I have learned have come from observing Life directly and using what we see to better organize our spaces and actions. I have learned these things from many places: from clients who refused to take "no hope" for an answer, from the Internet, prayers answered, professional colleagues, religious writings, scientific articles, and my own pets and their health issues. I learned some lessons from actions taken that were ineffective, even though experts considered them to be normal and proper. Some of these I now consider improper health care techniques. Yes, I have learned from my mistakes as well as my successes.

I readily admit that I am human and far from perfect, and I continue to strive to improve this work in progress that people call "Dr. P."

I am here to help each person I meet to become the best possible manifestation of his or her abilities and purposes. And what I observe is that when I do this best, people and their pets tend to be healthier and happier.

Sometimes miraculous things happen.

It has taken me more than fifty years to learn this stuff and put much of it into practice. There is still so much to learn that my head spins at times. My journey has been hard work. It should *not* take this much time for a health care professional to find this information and put it into practice. A major reason for my writing this book is to speed the flow of truth into our society.

We cannot afford for health care to be a mystery.

We cannot afford a society that waits for disease to emerge before it acts.

We cannot afford to use only drugs and surgery when other gentler and even more effective modalities exist. The world is a big and beautiful place, spinning at one thousand miles per hour. When traveling at that rate we simply do better when we have a correct map, right?

You are on a journey too. It is my most sincere hope that I can help you achieve your health care goals and in doing so help you and your loved ones to have the most wonderful life possible. Hopefully, if we travel together for a brief time we can each learn something from the other.

If you are reading this book you must have some interest in creating better health for your pet, yourself, and even your family. Let's begin our journey together by examining exactly what health is and how we can positively make the most of it and enjoy the experience.

Part 1.
The Basics of Health

"Liberty is the right to choose.
Freedom is the result of the
right choice."

Anonymous

Chapter 1. Your Pet's Miraculous Body

The Body's Systems

Your pet's body is absolutely miraculous. It is an extremely complex system that works in very simple and effective ways to achieve survival for itself and its offspring. Its ability to heal is far greater than most people suspect. Hopefully, by reading this book you will see that and be able to make better choices, and in turn enrich your life.

The body is comprised of creation and control systems that take energy, minerals, and water, and organize them into higher, more productive states of being.

One miracle of Life is that a puppy can eat dog food, drink water, breathe air, and become a dog. Basic physics and the laws of entropy are seriously stacked against any such system persisting. Material substances tend to flow from areas of higher concentration to lower ones. By all rights, our components should diffuse away from our bodies. But Life is clever and it has spent considerable planning on designing these bodies we all use. Dogs and cats obtain energy from eating other living things that ultimately obtained their energy directly from the sun's warming light beams. The body breaks down the chemical bonds that make up all molecules and uses the energy to drive its processes. It builds from supplies it obtains directly from the environment and manufactures a dizzying number of substances from vitamins, to hormones, to enzymes, and structural molecules.

The body is an interactive system that provides a safe space for biological processes to occur. Each part helps to secure that safe space, protect its integrity, and produce valuable products needed by the body to do its work. These products are exchanged for the mutual survival value with other cells and tissues. Each part also generates waste products and addresses threats in differing ways, and the body must handle these to maintain a safe space for Life processes to occur. Rapid deterioration and death result from failure in these systems.

The body achieves survival and health by these fascinating series of steps that make it look stable, when, in fact, it is nearly the ultimate in chaotic motion. If you consider these points as you read this book, you will begin to see how truly amazing bodies are and how incredible they are at achieving their goals. As you begin to better appreciate the difficult conditions we impose on bodies with our modern lifestyles, you will be even more amazed and respectful of how brilliant Life is in this design.

Life creates in patterns and if you examine a body, you will find all the systems that are present in larger living systems. Just as a healthy city contains a series of governmental bodies, a communications system, a police force, a fire department, a utility company, a waste management system, and a repair department, we find these same functions contained in every healthy body.

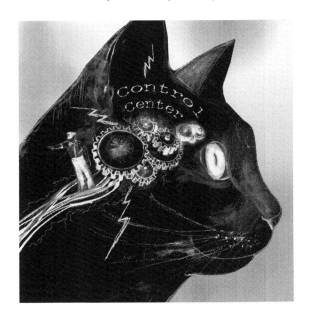

The brain contains upper-level control centers, which talk to lower-level control centers (such as acupuncture points and nerve centers in the bowel), and these communicate with local cellular control points. Communication flows through nerves and from other energy sources such as radio frequencies and light. Repair crews are ordered to do specific things each day and there are cells that work nearly exclusively to put out fires, arrest the growth of germs, and most importantly, clean the terrain of the body (clean biological terrain is very hard to damage or infect). Each of these functions is a part of our immune system, working to resist disease.

Frankly, as the table below demonstrates, we don't have an immune system, we are one. Our friends and neighbors can be viewed as part of our immune system.

No one person or thing survives alone; we survive best in cooperation.

Body Part	Immune Contribution
Skin	Provides a barrier to germs and chemicals, preserves water content, helps excrete toxins, heals itself after injury, communicates directly with the nervous and immune systems
Saliva	Has enzymes that block toxins and assist in digestion and antibodies that attack germs
Eyes	Allow for autonomic integration of the body's response to threats; tears wash out noxious substances and are antibacterial, antifungal, and antiviral
Nose	Warns of noxious substances, attracts the body to beneficial substances, traps particles and toxins, removes pathogens from the air
Brain and nerves	Coordinate actions by the various body parts
Stomach	Acid kills many pathogenic bacteria, fungi, and viruses; proper digestion of food prevents colonization by harmful organisms
Blood vessels	Carry nutrients, immune cells, immune substances, hormones, and other mediators to tissues; remove toxic or harmful substances
Lymph vessels and nodes	Carry intestinal tissue fluids back to circulation, transport immune cells, filter out and kill pathogenic organisms, return fluids and proteins to the circulatory system to prevent tissue swelling
Muscles and bones	Move the body toward good things and away from bad ones, remove larger dangerous objects, repair and maintain the body, harbor stem cells that produce many other aspects of the body's defenses

Table 1.1. Individual organ systems' contribution to the immune system. All parts of our bodies contribute in some way to the protective functions of our immune system.

Name a part of your body that is not part of the immune system and I'll give you a prize. Every part of you is focused on this immune function in one way or another. Each part of your pet's body is also directed with this specific purpose. The better our bodies function as immune systems, the healthier we will be.

If you really understand that, then you see why it is critical to take a "wholistic" view of health and healing: all of the parts are important to health, and the health of the body is more than just the sum of the health of the parts. If we make one part healthier, then the elements that depend upon that part improve. If we make a part less able to function, then the whole system fails to some degree by its reduced ability to perform its needed actions. Our pets get sick and get well according to these same rules. Feed them toxic food and their gastrointestinal systems are weakened. That compromises the immune cells that surround the intestines, which leads to the development of inflammation, infections, and allergies. If we make the intestine healthier by assisting digestion and improving the diet, then we also improve the status of the pet's immune system and lower its risk of disease. It really is that simple at its foundations.

You can work this backward as well. If we understand how biology solves problems, then we can imitate that process and often solve the most complex of problems in ways that don't cause further damage. As an example, when cities worked to solve pollution problems, they discovered that using a system similar to the body could help clean the water of dangerous waste. So we find that the body is very logical and effective at problem solving. The body is simply awesome when all of its parts are in communication and functioning according to their specific purposes. In fact, bodies knew how to solve these problems of living long before science was born. They are fundamentally bio-logical, that is to say, demonstrating Life's wisdom.

How the Systems Work

Life and its organisms solve these problems in ways that allow for better survival. Our genetic blueprint, the DNA, is actually a long record of successful ways of overcoming survival threats. Each part of the cell exists to handle some important function. The entire system is based on making things work and fixing things when they don't. Our living systems are wonderful examples of this.

Here's an example that demonstrates this simple but powerful truth. Most people are understandably terrified of cancer. Death rates from cancer are far too high and most of us know someone who has lost a pet or family member to the disease. Cancer appears to be striking at earlier ages, giving us more to worry about. Each day your pet's body forms more than ten thousand new cancer cells. While this seems like scary stuff, these abnormal cancer cells are regularly and rapidly handled by a normal immune system and never develop into tumors or spread to distant sites (a process called "metastasis," which is really why most cancer patients die). In other words, your pet can cure cancer and does so every day. In fact, you do too. And that is happy news worth sharing.

Every healthy body is immensely more effective than any oncologist (a doctor who specializes in treatment of cancer). The body uses its immune system to identify and correct or eliminate the cancer cells before they can spread and cause further damage. Your pet essentially has a surgery department that is more precise and capable than any hospital in the world. It can select and destroy single cells and repair spots on cell membranes to make them work better. It is only when the body's immune system is blocked or fails in some way that we need oncologists and other cancer treatment options.

This is truly miraculous and amazing.

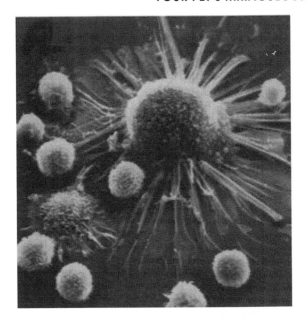

Figure 1.1. Immune cells surround and attack a cancer cell.
http://www.alternativecancer.net/images/cell_attack.jpg

So what happens to make this system break down? Why do nearly half our pets get cancer? The answer is discussed later in this book. For now, keep that question in your mind and realize how important it becomes to understand the normal operations of the body. (Hint: It has much to do with improper nutrition, chemical exposure, emotional stressors, and their combined effect on the integrity of the immune system.) Once we see how things work, we can better understand what happens as bodies begin to heal and we can better control our pets' health. This understanding makes us better animal stewards and helps us make better choices about our pets' health care, something we should be considering and doing long before cancer appears.

When people learn about cells and biochemistry, they often fail to look at the big picture and they get lost in the details. Actually, there is little reason to study something unless we can see how it is useful in our lives. Too much chemical detail just makes people yawn, so we won't do that here. You don't need to know the name of every molecule involved in the workings of your pet's body. However, it is essential that we communicate effectively and this requires some basic understanding on the part of everyone involved. As we later focus on the simple basics you'll find that this stuff is very logical and easy to understand.

Treating the Body and its Systems

Some people in our society depend upon sickness for their income. They fear anything that makes people healthy and they sometimes fight it rather viciously. The way to spot these people is to look at their results. Do their patients live longer, happier lives? Do they promote materials that result in a cure or do they promote technology that simply doesn't work? Do they use all manner of explanations to make it seem that the battle is hopeless? If so, then you will know whom you are addressing and can act accordingly.

Our present medical system, though it has made great strides, tends to concentrate mostly on diseases and disease states, and symptoms and symptom relief, rather than the normal systems that produce good health. This is a major problem in improving the health and care of people and pets. If we simply try to avoid diseases, we end up suppressing the symptoms without really understanding their meaning or how our body is trying to help us. In essence, we are defining health as the absence of symptoms rather than seeking a cure.

For example, if you go to a doctor and say, "My dog is vomiting," the treatment usually focuses on ways to stop the vomiting. But vomiting may be the correct action taken by your pet to remove damaging toxins, and suppressing that vomiting may actually lead to the toxins being deposited more deeply the dog's body. That, in turn, can lead to disease conditions that surface later in the dog's life. We may need to act if the vomiting is so severe that the dog can't maintain its hydration, but just suppressing the vomiting without understanding these factors is not necessarily good treatment.

> ... all drugs are potentially toxic and all have adverse effects associated with their use. How do we balance the proper use of these drugs with other alternative therapies? This is a major impulse driving the integrative health movement today.

In the case of itchy skin, doctors often control symptoms by administering drugs that block the chemicals causing the itch. This makes the dog stop itching and may make it more comfortable, but it doesn't cure the reason for the itch. If all we do is stop the itch by suppressing the body's normal response, then we have not healed anything. In fact, in many cases, we may have damaged our pet's body further with unseen chemical injuries. Later we will see how this can cause a pet's health to deteriorate and interfere with its ability to improve and stay well.

In recent years the media have been filled with disastrous news of severe and often fatal side effects of certain arthritis, weight loss, antidepressant, and diabetes medicines. Such reports have become so commonplace that most of us laugh at comedy sketches featuring products that promise a rapid relief in symptoms but carry the mandatory disclaimer of common side effects. Our radios, televisions, and computers constantly blare advertisements like this:

> "Gas got you down? Take Bloto for quick relief! Caution: Bloto's active ingredient megaloblotofarnine can cause hair loss, blinking, high blood pressure, and gonadal shrinkage. Diarrhea and vomiting were seen in 2 percent of patients. If bleeding occurs, cease usage and contact your doctor at once. Stroke and paralysis can occur with chronic usage."

We even see this with potato chips treated with abnormal fats that give the consumer an increased risk of diarrhea. To quote my six-year-old son, "Dad, why would I eat potato chips that could give me diarrhea?"

Exactly!

And why would I use a pharmaceutical medicine that could make me hemorrhage or damage my kidneys? Or destroy my pet's liver, alter its blood sugar, and make it more susceptible to diabetes? Or make it experience unpredictable violent behavior? Why indeed? Nevertheless, those side effects are commonly seen in prescriptions given every day in veterinary and medical practices across our country. An article in the *Journal of the American Medical Association* in 1998 revealed that each year about 106,000 Americans die and two million suffer severe adverse reactions to drugs prescribed in hospitals. This makes death from adverse drug effects the number four killer in this country. It is more difficult to obtain accurate data regarding the adverse effects of drugs and supplements on our pets because reporting of these reactions is not mandatory.

Death from adverse drug effects is a silent epidemic. Most people are unaware of the scope of this issue; so let's look at the numbers another way. Do you notice when a jet crashes, killing everyone on board? Of course you do.

Conversely, few realize that if a jumbo jet crashed every day of the year and killed all of the passengers in the process, that number would still be smaller than the number of people who die each year from adverse drug effects. This is a huge problem for our health care community to sort out and determine what can be done to decrease these tragedies that affect so many families each year.

Drug Type	Damage or Death From:
Chemotherapy	Loss of white blood cells and overwhelming infection
Anticoagulant	Fatal bleeding (gastrointestinal or intracranial)
Nonsteroidal anti-inflammatory	Intestinal bleeding, kidney failure, liver failure
Antidepressant	Suicide, drug interactions, arrhythmias, sudden death
Cardiovascular	Cardiac disturbance, organ failure, bleeding issues

Table 1.2. Human deaths from prescription drugs. Many adverse drug reactions are never reported. In human medicine one survey showed that drug-related deaths account for about 5 percent of all deaths in a hospital population. (Juntti-Patinen, Neuvonen. Drug-related deaths in a university central hospital. *European Journal of Clinical Pharmacology*. 2002.)

Recently, I consulted on a case involving an aged feline patient that developed severe kidney failure after being given a properly prescribed arthritis drug by another doctor. The clients couldn't believe that so many people would prescribe a drug that was so dangerous and not tell them about the possibility that their cat might end up needing more than $10,000 of dialysis.

Most patients treated with drugs are not going to die or have terrible side effects. Many of those deaths occur in critically sick individuals who would probably die if they were not placed on medication. Sometimes we need to use drugs, and in doing so we increase the life span and comfort levels of our patients. However, all drugs are potentially toxic and all have adverse effects associated with their use. How do we balance the proper use of these drugs with other alternative therapies? That question is driving the integrative health movement today.

One of the biggest problems that I see as I help people move toward better health is their total lack of knowledge about how bodies are put together and how they work. This knowledge is neither complex nor hard to understand, but it is vital to making health care choices. Many of these people have been told that medicine is simply too complex for them to grasp and that they are better off simply trusting doctors. This idea is a false one. Certainly doctors are well trained in many aspects of medicine, but no single doctor knows everything. Except in emergencies, everyone should take time to understand what is being done to as well as for patients, and owners really should know the negative aspects of their pets' treatment plans.

Pet owners must strive for better understanding if they are to participate effectively as members of their pets' health care team. Doctors and health care teams must embrace this idea and do all they can to help clients understand their pets' health care issues. When people begin to see how beautiful and powerful this knowledge really is, they begin to take better steps toward improved health. Sadly, most of us have been poorly educated about health. It can be an unpleasant surprise to discover how much false data we have absorbed from advertising and poor education. The best way to improve our understanding is simply to seek out and find the true information (which stands out because it works). We can better align ourselves with correct information when we find false information and remove it from our thinking. The reward is better lives for all! And that is biological.

> *It is through true understanding that we can achieve more control of our pets' health care.*

☆ ☆ ☆

Chapter 2. A Case of Improving Health

Judy Blue Eyes

Theories and philosophy are great, but now it's time to look at how this information can help our pets recover from diseases and live healthy. Is there a theory or philosophy that, when applied, leads to better health? Let's examine a real case from our office and see what we can learn from one person's journey to improved health for her beloved cat.

If I showed you this picture (Figure 2.1) would you say this cat is healthy or not?

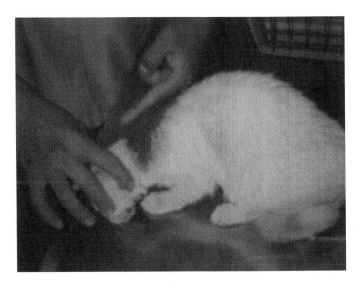

Figure 2.1. Judy Blue Eyes on her initial presentation for care.
Notice the size and inflammation involved in this lesion.

What do you see? Judy had a bad sore on her back. Pretty scary, isn't it?

Judy Blue Eyes presented to our office as a seven-year-old female spayed cat that had developed a nasty ulcerated sore on her back. It had persisted for several months and not responded to the best efforts of several very competent veterinarians. Treatment with symptom-suppressing antibiotics and steroids had made no difference and the sore was getting worse. A specialist from a veterinary school felt that this lesion was likely a tumor and had discussed putting Judy Blue Eyes to sleep.

Fortunately, her owner decided to seek out an integrative approach and brought Judy Blue Eyes to our office. Her examination showed an extensive sore, but no evidence of fleas or other parasites. Special tests were done to detect fungal infections, bacterial infections, and other parasites, but none were revealed. Her blood tests were normal. We discussed doing a biopsy, a test to see if cancer or inflammation was present, but Judy's caregiver was dead set against the surgery.

I told her this was a difficult case. I could promise nothing, but in many cases such conditions are caused by toxins that have accumulated in the body. Sometimes we can assist chronic disease patients by using homeopathic medicines that assist the body in removing these toxins. It would be long and hard work, but I was willing if she was interested, and since Judy Blue Eyes was happy and didn't seem to be in pain I couldn't really justify euthanasia. Judy Blue Eyes' human "mom" was relieved and opted for this experimental alternative medical treatment.

Judy's examination said the following things to me:
1. "I have energy and vitality."
2. "I have an appetite and normal excretions."

3. "I have the ability to grow skin and maintain healthy skin in other parts of my body, and this part used to be normal."
4. "My body is working to accomplish something and is working very hard on that job."
5. "I am trying to get healthy!"

Judy's severe inflammation took lots of work to produce, and the body would not allow it to heal, so it must have been associated with some bigger job the body was involved in doing.

Homotoxins and Homeopathy

> Dr. Reckeweg realized that all disease symptoms result from intentional efforts by the body to handle homotoxins.

This approach to healing originated with a German physician, Hans-Heinrich Reckeweg, who stated that all disease is the body's attempt to isolate, remove, or excrete substances he called "homotoxins" (an abbreviated word from *Homo sapiens* and toxins; homotoxins are things that are toxic to humans). Reckeweg saw that all disease symptoms are the result of intentional efforts by the body to handle these homotoxins. Because his own father had been saved from kidney failure with homeopathic medicines, Dr. Reckeweg worked tirelessly to develop a system of healing called "Homotoxicology." He refined the use of low-dose agents to drain these toxins from the body and stimulate healing of organs and tissues.

What Is Homeopathy?

Homeopathy is a natural form of healing to gently stimulate the body's natural defense mechanisms. Substances used in homeopathy are researched or proven, a process involving volunteers ingesting toxins and recording their symptoms. When we administer very small amounts of these substances we find that they treat symptoms that match these "provings." Homotoxicology uses combinations of these compounds in low concentrations to activate a patient's natural defenses.

In Judy's case this translated into a homeopathic combination of medicine, nutritional therapy to support her immune system, and an antibiotic. Antibiotics had been used before with no benefit, but this time Judy immediately stopped itching for two weeks, something her owner was very pleased to report because she had not stopped itching since the condition arose months before. Judy Blue Eyes began to improve and her nasty lesion finally started to heal. I cautioned that although I was happy, I knew that the body had more to show us in this case. I explained that frequently this was a great sign but it also indicated that the body was building strength and that soon it would attack the condition more aggressively. It was important for everyone to know this so that the body could begin to really heal the area. Imagine the confusion that arises when someone doesn't know this important fact about natural healing. If this is not known, it is so easy in traditional medicine to just begin prescribing one drug after another in an attempt to resolve the condition. Each new drug becomes a toxin that the body must work even harder to eliminate, and the repeated suppression makes it even harder for a patient to recover.

As expected, a few days later things got interesting as Judy Blue Eyes' itching became much more severe. Her human mom was worried, but I was excited because we frequently see itching worsen as the body begins to repair diseased tissue. Inflammation is like a bonfire that the body uses to "burn up" homotoxins from the tissue. We discussed this and then stopped using the antibiotic, an important step because the antibiotic could suppress healing in this case, due to its adverse effect on cellular energy production.

Enzymes are complex proteins that help the body perform many tasks, including healing. We suspected that Judy Blue Eyes' enzyme systems were already blocked, a common condition in patients with chronic, nonhealing diseases and patients who have been treated with antibiotic or anti-inflammatory drugs. We used other homeopathic agents to help unblock these necessary elements of healing and improve her ability to make energy. Much to my relief, Judy Blue Eyes began to heal quickly after receiving homeopathic agents that assist cellular energy production.

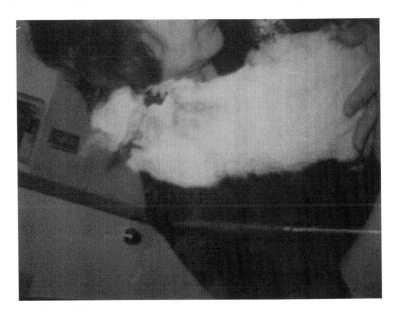

Figure 2.2. Judy Blue Eyes after a month of natural and integrative therapy. The wound is healing nicely at this time.

Not all of our cases recover so remarkably, but when we find truth, healing begins, and when healing is occurring, we know we are on the right track. Judy's progress was exciting, indeed. Figure 2.2 shows her wound after a month. Judy made a full and complete recovery. She has had no further recurrences and continues to live happily. We advised Judy's mom to avoid toxic chemicals whenever possible and to never vaccinate this cat again because the lesion was in a site commonly used for vaccination with a vaccine containing herpes virus, a disease that might be associated with skin problems. This was a sensible recommendation because Judy is an indoor cat, and now everyone is happy.

This was a great case.

> # When we find Truth, then healing begins, and when healing is occurring, we know we are on the right track.

Judy Blue Eyes has instructed many people about natural medicine in lectures across the United States, and she gave me confidence to more actively pursue biological therapy and eventually coauthor a textbook for veterinarians who are interested in learning how to integrate these natural therapies into their practices. I owe her much for her help and her recovery.

Understanding Health and Healing

Below are nine important lessons regarding health care. Bookmark this page and refer to it while your pet is undergoing treatment because it will greatly help you navigate the process.

1. Living things are organized to survive. They constantly expend energy in ways that lead to improved survival. Sometimes conditions that persist are the body's way of trying to solve some other problem. Disease signs are communications for the doctor and client to decode. Once this decoding has occurred, proper therapy can begin and hopefully recovery follows.

2. Diseases and symptoms of disease are actually the body's efforts to handle homotoxins. This effort can take many forms: excretion of waste through tears, vomiting, diarrhea, mucus, sweat, or various other bodily excretions; destruction of homotoxins by inflammation; storage and deposition of homotoxins while the body attempts to find a way to handle them; and transformation of homotoxins by metabolic enzymes and cellular energy. As toxins persist and do further damage, the body develops more chronic diseases, and these we often name (diabetes, high blood pressure, heart disease, arthritis, etc.). Cancer can result from deeply damaged cellular terrain and subsequent destruction of the normal genetic material of the cell.

3. Giving the body clean air, water, and food, and providing it with agents that assist in removing homotoxins can lead to reversal of disease signs and symptoms. Not all disease is curable, but many chronic forms improve when approached in this way. Symptoms occur as the body eliminates toxins and repairs its

tissues. They also tell us that the body needs further assistance.

4. Using low doses of certain compounds has a stimulatory effect on the body. This is the principle used in homeopathic medicine.

5. Larger amounts of certain compounds can also stimulate cellular function, which is the principle behind nutritional medicine as well as certain drug treatments.

6. Large amounts of compounds can suppress functions, and sometimes this is needed to manage medical emergencies such as infections. This is how antibiotics function, but when they are used long term they can harm the body through their toxic actions. This knowledge allows for doctors to administer biologically friendly therapeutic agents following antibiotic therapy to reduce the harm they may have caused to the body's immune system.

7. Doctors often do not know what is going to happen with a case, so it is critical that the doctor, patient, and client communicate throughout the process. If positive change is occurring, then change nothing. Be patient. Just because one doctor fails to resolve a condition does not mean that it is incurable. No doctor knows every possible therapy for every case, and euthanasia is not needed just because a patient fails to recover fully. Getting second opinions and listening to your innate sense of Truth can lead you to better health for your pet.

8. Getting better is a process and it can take time, sometimes a lifetime. Sometimes symptoms worsen, and often this is necessary for a full recovery. Suppressing such signs can stop healing and prevent recovery.

9. Healing is the manifestation of love. Fear, among other things, blocks healing. If we increase our love and dedicate ourselves to finding Truth, then healing can begin, and in healing we always have Truth. This is why we always say, "Seek Truth, and healing follows."

When you first looked at the pictures of Judy Blue Eyes on her initial visit, you likely thought she looked unhealthy. But what is health really? In our office we view health as a state of existence wherein the parts of the organism function adequately to achieve its goals and purposes. In health, the organism can attain survival.

Health implies "wholeness" or "completeness." As we consider this we begin to realize that health is not something, it is a state of "somethings" manifested in the totality of the patient's existence. We also see it as a dynamic, constantly changing condition. Think about the health of your body yesterday, a few minutes ago, and several years ago, and you will note differences. We all know about waking up and feeling less than energetic one day and better the next. Health is a state of existence that manifests itself in various ways at different times. Disease symptoms are actually healthy methods that our bodies use to get our attention. Symptoms need understanding, not suppression. Discomfort is a warning that we are treading on more dangerous ground. We all have some experience of doing something and then feeling poorly afterward. We ingest too much rich food, consume alcohol to excess, or even just eat too much fat or sugar, which can make us feel rotten. Clearly, we can affect our health by the choices we make. And we can direct healing by making different choices as well.

The good news is that there are things we can do to improve health too. When we do this, the body has built-in rewards that make us feel even better. However, when we ignore our bodies or miss their messages, sometimes getting healthier can result in unpleasant feelings. If we stop exercising and then start again, we can expect some muscle stiffness as the body responds to increased demands and begins repairing and reinforcing stressed structures. This is normal and these unpleasant feelings tend to pass as healing repairs the damage and builds healthier systems in the body. What we use gets stronger and what we ignore fades away. This means that health can be improved or worsened. It follows that we can often do things to improve health, and isn't that is the purpose of medicine?

> *We can do things to improve health in many situations, and that is the purpose of medical activities, isn't it?*

Chapter 3. Evaluating Your Pet's Health

Look and Learn

Evaluating health means looking at signs and deciding how they relate. It includes perceiving and valuing the information we have regarding our pet's health. As a steward charged with making choices for your pet's health care, you must develop some understanding of health so that you can value what you see, smell, and feel.

Look at your pet. What do you see right away?

- ❑ How does it look? Does it stand up tall with bright eyes, shining coat, and vitality screaming from every pore? Is the tail wagging or hanging loose?
- ❑ Does it have fresh breath and even smell good? Are the teeth nice and white with pink gums, or are they stained?
- ❑ How is its appetite? Does your pet eat quickly and happily? Has it changed the way it approaches the food bowl? Does it walk to the bowl, look, and then walk away without eating?
- ❑ Is it thin, normal weight, or obese?
- ❑ Look at the skin. Do you see sores? Red spots? Hair loss in large areas or in patches? Is there a foul odor? Is the coat dry or greasy? Does your pet lick or groom or pull out its hair excessively? Are there brown stains on the feet or legs?

- ❏ Is the muzzle hair going gray?
- ❏ What about physical ability? Can your pet play as long as it desires or does it slow down or refuse to play?
- ❏ Does your pet have an appetite and eat well? Is it eating more or less than usual?
- ❏ How are the stools? Are they regular and formed? Or are they loose and smelly? (OK, all poop is smelly but some is just downright nasty.) Do you see worms in the stool?
- ❏ How much water does your pet drink? Is it drinking more than usual on a daily basis? Is the water bowl empty? Does your pet "pray" at the water bowl, staying there drinking for long periods of time?
- ❏ Can your pet hold its urine all night or do you have to let it out more often than before? Does the urine smell foul? Are ants attracted to where your pet urinates?
- ❏ How do these observations compare to those of yesterday, last week, and a few years ago? Does it seem like your pet is looking better and better, or is it deteriorating?

You have just begun to evaluate your pet's health. Noticing and evaluating changes in a pet and bringing those to the attention of the veterinarian are the most important things an owner can do after providing a safe space with good nutrition and clean water. These observations, by pet owners, veterinarians, and veterinary technicians, are the basis for a health evaluation. Even though you, the owner, may not have professional training, you do know your pet, and noticeable changes can lead your doctor to important findings that help to determine a correct treatment plan.

> Noticing and evaluating changes in a pet and bringing those to the attention of the veterinarian are the most important things an owner can do after providing a safe space with good nutrition and clean water.

Trust your observations and intuition, and seek professional care if your attention sticks on something. You are a pretty amazing biological system and have the purpose of being a good caregiver. That purpose, coupled with your perceptions, often leads you to fixate on something or feel anxious about it, which is a good reason to call a professional and have your pet's health evaluated. As a veterinarian, I am constantly amazed by the accuracy of client observations. Even when owners incorrectly "guess" at a suspected diagnosis, they are usually correct in their suspicion that the pet needs a professional evaluation. Once we conduct the correct diagnostic processes, more often than not we find problems when clients feel there is something wrong with their pets.

In fact, we don't have to wait until a pet is so very sick to make a clear medical diagnosis to begin the health care process. It just doesn't make sense to wait for full-blown illness when there are many things we can do to improve the health of our pets. Disease prevention is an acceptable consideration, but I prefer to think in terms of taking steps to create health. When pets are truly ill, we need to identify the factors associated with their dis-ease (not at ease), but truthfully, the disease occurs only because of a loss of health. Focusing our attention on creating health is much more beneficial than fighting disease.

The Veterinarian's Perspective

Let me talk a bit about how veterinarians address health problems. If a medical problem is occurring in the body, we need information to better understand its cause so we can act appropriately. Once we recognize the cause we can act more effectively to return the pet to optimal health.

We need to study your pet's health and find departures from its ideal condition. We begin by looking and asking. We do an examination and obtain a good health history. Interestingly, the words "examine" and "study" both originate from older words that literally mean "to look." The ability to see clearly is critical to maintaining health and recovering health when it has been lost. Obstacles that prevent us from looking accurately are enemies of healing; they can actually prevent recovery.

In alternative medicine we speak a lot about perceptions and looking. During the history part of an examination appointment, we look at the pet's life and find out if there is anything that might predispose it to a particular form of disease. We learn where the pet lives, where it lived previously, where it travels, who or what interacts with the pet, its diet and activity, its vaccine history, and other factors that are critical to reaching a diagnosis and beginning a correct treatment plan.

> The word "diagnosis" comes from word roots that mean "to look through and know." This means that we make a diagnosis by looking at factors and then determining the most likely cause of the condition.

One part of this looking process is to learn if there was a time when the disease state did not exist and then carefully go forward in time to determine whether any factors can be identified as responsible for the pet's loss of health. In some such cases we may be able to rapidly change the pet's health. For example, a dog that is very healthy goes to a barbeque and then begins to vomit afterward. We first want to know what the dog was fed or stole from someone's plate at the party. This could well be the entire problem that needs to be corrected.

The word "diagnosis" comes from word roots that mean "to look through and know," which means that to reach a diagnosis we need to look at factors and then determine the most likely cause or causes of the condition. Doctors make diagnoses, but clients should as well. And if the discovery by the doctor, client, and patient, all working together, agree, then we often see the best examples of healing manifested.

In medicine we often talk about a patient's condition. Did you know that the roots of the word "condition" mean "what we have agreed with," and so seeing where the pet has been and what it has done gives us vital information about what sorts of problems may be involved. The word "study" also means simply "to look," so to study or diagnose your pet requires that the veterinarian look at things in a variety of ways. A medical test is just a way to look at your pet's body to learn more about how things are operating.

Modern medicine has a massive number of tools for looking at particular aspects of your pet's health. Below are just a few of the commonly used tools:

- ❑ Direct physical examination with our five senses: Allows us to view your pet in its current condition and compare the findings to what is considered normal. Smells, sights, and sounds are all important for diagnosing a condition.

❏ Magnification and optics systems: Allow us to see things we otherwise couldn't without assistance. We can use lenses to examine the eyes, ears, and skin, and we can examine the interior through fiber optics systems that transmit images to a television screen where they can be magnified and examined more closely.

❏ Examination of bodily fluids such as stool, urine, or pus: Can further assist in the search for disease causes.

❏ Biopsy and cytology: Abnormal tissue can be examined with a microscope for evidence of infection, inflammation, allergy, immune imbalance, and cancer.

❏ Culture and sensitivity: Allow us to determine which bacteria and fungi are present and determine which antibiotic or antifungal agents are most likely to be effective.

❏ X-rays and CT scans: Also called "radiographs" or "CAT scans," these let us look inside our pets to see things such as organ changes and bone injuries.

❏ Ultrasound: Gives us another way to examine a pet's interior using very safe and noninvasive sound waves. Ultrasound can demonstrate tumors, organ thickening, blood clots, and many other problems.

❏ MRI scans: MRI uses magnetic resonance to generate very detailed images. These are commonly used by specialists to image sinuses, skull, brain, spinal cord, and extremities.

❏ Electrocardiograms: Examine the heart's electrical activity.

❏ Blood testing: Tells us what is happening biochemically and cellularly inside your pet. Evidence of some diseases appears only on blood tests.

Test Name	Purpose	Benefits	Weaknesses
Stool examination for parasites	Detects intestinal parasites.	Allows for use of correct medication in treating the correct condition.	Does not detect all parasites and may give false negative results because parasite eggs are not seen.
Blood titers	Detect antibodies to indicate the immune response.	Evaluate vaccine protection; diagnose diseases caused by various infections and parasites.	During initial infection the tests may not detect antibody and give false negative results.
Skin scrape	Detects mites.	Finding the parasite allows for selection of correct medication by the doctor.	Mites can be buried deep in the skin and may not show on the test; multiple scrapings may be needed.
Cytology	Identify disease state for diagnosis and prognosis.	Knowing the cells present gives clues about the disease process that is present and the pet's chances of recovery in some cases.	Can't always identify the cause of a condition; may give misleading results in some cases.
Blood count	Understand the condition of blood cells.	Helps identify infections, stresses, and blood cancers or other problems.	Not all infections or tumors cause abnormal cell counts.
Blood chemistries	Assist in diagnosis and prognosis, and in monitoring treatment results.	Identify where stress or malfunction is occurring in the body; assist in choosing medications for effect/safety.	Disease may not be severe enough to cause abnormalities; sometimes a diagnosis cannot be made.
X-rays	Penetrate the body to see inside.	Help identify tumors, fractures, sprains, infections, and organ diseases.	May not show certain things until the disease is much more advanced.
MRI/CT scans	Provide better images inside the body.	Help to view inside organs for better diagnosis.	Vary in which issues are seen best; expensive.
Ultrasound	See inside the body without radiation.	Identifies many abnormalities; can be used to direct other tests such as biopsy and cytology.	Not all issues can be seen on ultrasound; not good for bones or places with air/gas.
Endoscopy	Uses optics to look inside the body.	Allows the doctor to look directly at diseased tissues and get better samples for biopsy and other evaluations.	Requires anesthesia in most cases; not all diseases can be identified; damage and organ rupture can occur but are rare.

Table 3.1. Commonly performed veterinary diagnostic tests and their strengths and weaknesses. ("Prognosis" is the prediction of good or bad outcomes in a particular disease.)

Some tests can be used as part of a preventive health program. Having your pet's stool and/or blood checked regularly for parasites protects them as well as your family and your neighbors' pets from parasitism. All pets should have routine checks for stool parasites each year. Checking blood levels of antibody can prevent vaccine-related illness by allowing pets to receive fewer vaccines. Older pets should be blood tested regularly to monitor their organ function and blood pressure. These are all very important tests that greatly assist your doctor in deciding what your pet needs.

Most veterinary experts agree that pets over eight to ten years of age should be examined and monitored for health at least every six months. Because pets age faster than humans, having an exam every six months is like you or me seeing our doctor every three to four years. For older people and pets this is a really good idea. The table below shows commonly used tests and their benefits and shortcomings.

These tests help you and your doctor to communicate with your pet's system and gain important information that can be used to identify specific problems, arrive at a correct diagnosis, identify which treatments may be needed, and predict your pet's chances of recovery (prognosis). Proper use of diagnostic tests greatly increases our chances of helping a sick pet and can be very helpful in identifying illnesses before they become too severe to treat successfully. This is particularly important when dealing with very young or very old pets.

Following the history and examination, your doctor may recommend tests and you should feel free to ask sufficient questions to understand why these are being done, what benefit they can provide, and what you can expect after the testing. Tests can greatly assist you in your desire to identify and improve your pet's health and they help your doctor do his or her part in this effort.

> *If there is a problem in the body we need information to better understand its cause so we can act appropriately. Once the cause is recognized, we can act more effectively to return your pet to optimal health.*

✵ ✵ ✵

Chapter 4: Asking Your Pet for Assistance

Seeking Answers

Being a veterinarian is a dream come true for me. Nothing gives me greater joy than seeing people smiling happily with their healthy pets. There is something about this unconditional and unlimited love that just makes me tingle all over. Going into an exam room to find a pet that is emitting vitality from every pore and an owner who appreciates this just gets me through my days with a smile on my face.

I graduated from one of the top clinical veterinary schools in the United States. I was well prepared to take on my role in healing, and I began practicing in 1983. I found that the approach I was taught worked well for many patients, but sometimes I would do everything right, perform all the correct tests, and still not have a clue why a particular patient was not doing better. This really frustrated me. When I complained about this I was told, "Hey, buddy boy, the world is far from perfect and you are not God. Get over it and get back to doing what you can to change things."

In a superficial way, that comment made sense to me. After all, I am not God and I can't wave my hands and discover things that are hidden from view. If I had done all that could be done and I failed, it was normal to feel sorry for the client. But what else could I do? It was for other people in academics or research, whose jobs were to find better diagnostics and better information through research, so we clinicians could do more and be more successful. Our profession was doing that, so why worry more?

The answer to that is pretty obvious. All a person who loves animals and people needs do is look once into the eyes of an owner being told by the veterinarian why he or she doesn't know what is wrong and can't explain or come up with better treatment. The look of fear and emptiness is not pleasant, and it is certainly not the effect I hoped to create as a professional. I simply couldn't stand not being able to do more for my patients when they needed more. Frankly, it has been that single force that has driven me deeper and deeper into holistic therapies.

In 1983, when I graduated from veterinary school at Colorado State University, if you had asked me to buy a machine that nearly always worked and would direct me precisely to treatments that would help patients recover, it would have been a pretty easy sale to get me to buy the thing. I would have been really impressed to learn that such a machine didn't need an electrical hookup or even batteries. What professional wouldn't want instant access to correct information about a patient's body and the treatment that would make it healthier? Medical equipment catalogues are filled with various devices and tests to assist us in this mission. Every one of these machines has weaknesses, but they help us in some way in our mission to better understand what our patients need.

But what if I told you that your pet's own body was this most remarkable device? Would you be interested to find out that your pet could expertly advise us directly about which organs are undergoing stress, which tissues need help, and which agents are more likely to assist in recovery of health? What if this procedure even told you which things might cause bad reactions in your pet's condition?

Holy cow! That sounds like science fiction, but it is a scientific fact, and people who know about muscle response testing usually just smile and nod in agreement about the wonderful tool available to anyone who is willing to learn a new technique. I believe that in the future this form of treatment evaluation will become widespread. It simply helps too much to keep it bottled up.

Muscle Response Testing

Dr. Goodheart, a chiropractor who observed the basic phenomena of Muscle Response Testing (MRT) and began developing it for use in his clinical practice, first discussed and developed the basic technique. The basic principle is incredibly simple–if we place a substance that is good for the body on the body, the body somehow recognizes this and it becomes stronger (if the nervous system is functioning properly). Likewise, if we place things that are harmful to the body on the body, then the body becomes weaker. This change is instant. It is repeatable.

MRT does not require belief in spirits or alternative medicine for this to work. In fact, sometimes skeptics are amazed that it works whether one believes or not. It is simply a biological principle as predictable as gravity and as natural for a doctor to do as feeling a pulse or taking a respiratory rate. If the nervous system is properly functioning, muscle strength changes when the body contacts various substances. More than 95 percent of people and animals can be muscle tested when they are properly prepared. It is remarkable to find a tool to help evaluate health in 95 percent of patients without special machinery, radiation, invasion of the body, or pain.

Wow, that is just a wonderful tool for us all!

But you don't have to take my word for this. You can test it out for yourself. For most people it is pretty easy to test.

Remember that some people's nervous systems are not functioning normally (they are "blocked" or "switched"), so this doesn't work for everyone. That said, at least eight out of ten will respond to the following two tests:

> You are just observing whether there is a change. This helps demonstrate the presence of a basic biological principle–some things make a strong muscle stronger and some things make it weaker.

First test:

1. Have a friend stand up and extend his arm. Make sure he is not crossing his legs or feet. Tell him to match your pressure as you take your open hand and press down gently on his wrist. Do NOT grasp his wrist firmly. Do not press hard; just press hard enough to see if he has a strong muscle (that is one that can match your pressure). This is not a contest of strength. If the person is so weak that he cannot hold his arm against your push, this test can't be done because he needs attention to make the muscle strong enough to test. That is a job for a professional and is not part of this demonstration.

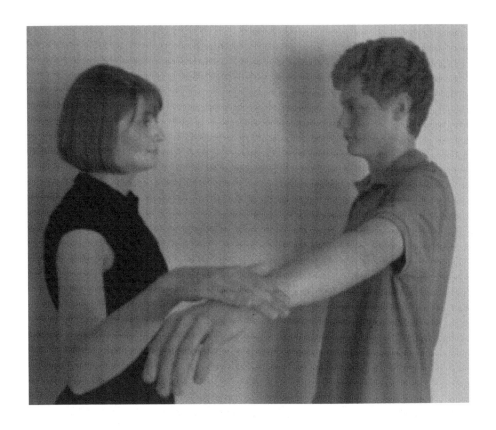

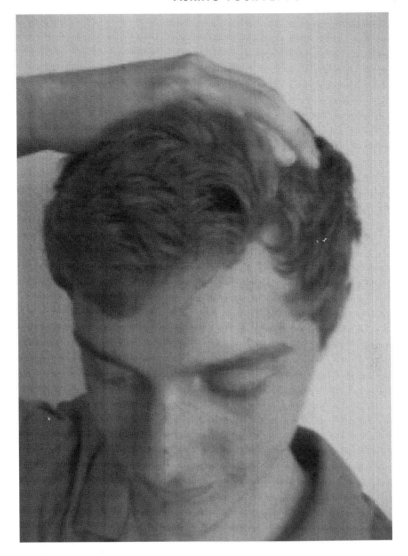

2. Have a person with a strong muscle place his hand on the top of his head while you test the other arm extended, as above.

3. Have him turn his hand over. Generally, most people are stronger on one side than the other. It isn't important which one or why it occurs, just observe the effect.

What happened? Did you do it on several people? What did you observe? Is there a connection or phenomenon that you found?

Second test:

1. Have a friend stand up and hold his arm extended. Tell him to match your pressure as you take your open hand and press down gently on his wrist. Do NOT grasp his wrist firmly. Do not press hard; just press hard

enough to see if he has a strong muscle. Again, this is not a contest of strength. If the person is so weak that he cannot hold his arm against your push down, this test can't be done because he needs attention to make the muscle strong enough to test.

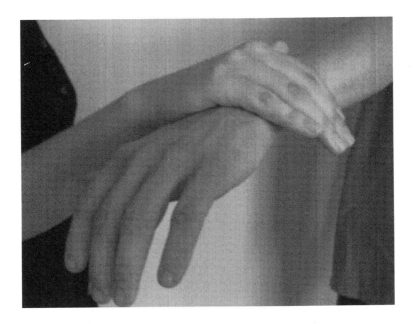

2. Repeat this test while having the person hold white sugar on his chest. Did he lose muscle strength?
3. You can try this with several other items such as alcoholic drinks, milk, tobacco, cheese, eggs, cleaning fluids, artificial sweeteners, cosmetics, etc. Just note what happens.

Hopefully you have found what most people discover— that something happens in these tests. If you have seen that, then you can understand that Muscle Response Testing detects some biological principle. If not, it isn't necessary to see these things, but it does help. If your doctor does muscle testing you can ask for another demonstration, but often the best way to learn about this procedure is simply to have it done. There is nothing like the face of someone who goes weak the first time a stressed organ is located and then goes strong on application of a nutritional agent. It is simply very impressive for most people.

Our doctors use a specific protocol of MRT that gets most people and animals to a condition in which they can be tested accurately. It is called Nutrition Response Testing℠. It is a simple, painless procedure that consists of a few basic steps. First, the doctor specially trained in the technique locates a strong muscle. If no strong muscle is found the doctor assesses several factors and makes adjustments until one appears. Once these are handled the muscle will usually become stronger and can be used for testing. The regulation of the nervous system is then checked (if a patient doesn't respond correctly, the doctor must find out why and correct that before further testing can occur). Other factors are evaluated and the doctor proceeds until the patient responds in a predictable fashion. Now the actual testing can begin.

The doctor presses on various sites on the body in areas attached by nervous tissue to major organs. Weakness is noted. After assessing the entire body the doctor prioritizes weak organ responses to determine which organ needs help first. That organ is assessed and nutritional, herbal, and homeopathic agents are tested to determine what is needed to strengthen the reflex. Useful agents will instantly correct the reflex being examined. Many therapeutic agents are tested until the reflexes are balanced properly. Further tests are completed to determine the pet's ability to take the supplements and digest them. After that the pet simply takes the agents and returns in several days or weeks for a follow-up evaluation.

Over time, a patient's condition begins to improve or changes are made in an effort to help the body move toward healing. The doctor and owner work together, guided by the wisdom of the pet's own body and its brilliant regulatory and control systems. This is exciting and transformational work for all involved.

Imagine how empowering it can feel to realize that you and your pet both have a brilliant system right inside your bodies that wants you to get well and is working hard to get your attention so that it can guide you toward better health.

It is important to understand that Muscle Response Testing and Nutrition Response Testing are not done for diagnosis. People can get confused about this, and that can lead to trouble. Muscle Response Testing can often reveal disease or functional weakness in organs, even before other conventional tests show the condition. But it is not a diagnostic procedure. MRT helps your doctor understand which organs are weak and what nutritional support reduces those stressors. It even helps your doctor determine where therapy should begin for the best effect. However, if normal diagnostic tests aren't conducted, important information may be overlooked. For example, a pet with a hidden tumor may present for Muscle Response Testing and be found to have a weak thymus (an important part of the immune system), or it could have a weak spleen or liver. Chemical stressors, and possibly viruses, are located. The nutritional support that is prescribed to support those organs helps the body, but it does not necessarily address the greater threat of the tumor hiding inside. To find that tumor, we need diagnostic tests such as x-rays, blood work, ultrasound examinations, CT scans, MRIs, and even surgery.

Fopster

I think this is very neat stuff. So let's look a real case in which MRT was used successfully to assist the doctor in guiding therapy.

"Fopster" was a healthy one-year-old miniature poodle. She was spayed and lived in a wonderful, supportive home. She ate a premium dog food and received regular home-prepared meals including fresh raw vegetables and meat. Her owner brought her to our clinic because her behavior had changed and her energy had suddenly decreased. Instead of jumping up to play, she preferred to stay in her bed well after her normal wake-up time.

Her owner was rightfully concerned and presented her for an examination in our clinic. She did appear less "bright" than usual. Her eyes were just a bit duller and she didn't respond as playfully as normal. Nevertheless, no major findings were present on her examination. When I tested her for muscle strength I found that she had no strong muscles for reference. We did some detective work and found that she was muscle testing for the presence of a chemical toxicity. A nutritional supplement that made the muscle strong was located and we continued with testing and found that most of her organ stress was centered in her small intestine and liver. The muscle test indicated that the most important organ was the liver. Two simple whole food supplements strengthened the reflex and were chosen for her treatment program.

When your pet is sick, or "not quite right," there are tests that can be done to help find the area of stress and determine supplements that may support your pet before a more severe disease arises.

Fopster still looked a bit ill and since her mom was worried, we decided to do a diagnostic blood test, which revealed that Fopster was suffering from liver inflammation. The blood test had no way of determining why the liver was inflamed, or what was causing the inflammation, but this was consistent with the muscle testing, so we advised the owner to see how Fopster felt in a few days.

Fopster had become ill a few days after massive wildfires began burning in Los Angeles and San Diego, California. The toxic smoke was everywhere. When homes burn they release very toxic waste products into the air, and more than one thousand homes had burned that week. Like humans, animals inhale these toxins, and their livers, kidneys, and respiratory and digestive systems work to eliminate the toxins. During this time we saw many patients with active liver disease of a minor degree, and many of these patients recovered on very simple therapy plans involving gentle nutrition, healthy food, lots of clean water, and bathing to remove the toxins from the pet's coat (they lick, you know, and thus ingest massive amounts of these toxins).

Fopster was running and playing again in two days and her liver tests were normal a week later. Her liver weakness disappeared on MRT. I was happy because the two types of testing revealed that her condition was minor and so we could proceed with less fear and worry while she did her healing work and recovered.

Fopster's case was a simple one. Later we will look at more complex and interesting cases, but for now just realize that when your pet is sick or just not right, there are tests that can be done to help find the area of disease and support that area before more severe disease arises. We call this treating functional disease–those conditions that are not so severe as to be named as official diseases but still have a negative effect on the patient's comfort and ease of survival.

While muscle testing can never give a medical diagnosis, it does allow us to ask the body a question and then assist the body in answering that question so that a doctor can build a better treatment plan. Once we know what the body is asking for, we can often begin to better understand the precise mechanisms that are occurring to create the disease state. That is powerful medicine. MRT is another way to locate and use the truth and power contained in biological systems. As a doctor, I find muscle response testing to be a particularly powerful tool in seeking truth and promoting healing.

Seek truth and healing follows. Anything that promotes healing contains truth and is part of medicine. Your pet's body knows truth and wants you to find it.

✳ ✳ ✳

Chapter 5. Nutrition:
The Foundation of Health

Emphasis on Quality

"Yes, we are not only digging our graves with our teeth, but we are well on the way to killing ourselves with our stupidity..." Phil Bate, PhD.

The quote above is from a professional who is well known for his work in getting people off toxic psychiatric medications and assisting them through nutritional therapy. If a body is missing essential nutrients, it can't repair itself and therefore feels depressed or less lively. Many cases of so-called "depression" are actually nutritional imbalances. Supplements like omega-3 oils can actually work as well as pharmaceuticals in human patients suffering from these problems. Likewise, if our pets' diets are inadequate, then it is easy to see how nutritional deficiencies could lead to disease. A diet that is missing essential nutrients fails to provide the building blocks and raw materials that the body needs, so it is forced to adapt and make its best efforts at survival with inadequate materials.

Too much nutrition can cause illness and disease as well. There are good reasons why the overweight cat to the right is worried. Research clearly shows that obesity robs pets of two years of their healthy time of life and one year of life itself. "Over-nutrition" rapidly leads to elevated hormone levels, excess fat storage, and sugar infiltration of essential body proteins. Toxic doses of chemical vitamins can lead to liver and bone damage. Cancer is even linked to obesity. None of those things are good.

Most of us learned about nutrition in our basic health classes. But many people really don't fully understand that proper nutrition is more than just eating the right foods and popping the right multivitamin pill. In many ways our health and the health of our pets has been silently stolen from us by common practices of food companies and modern agriculture. We are under attack biologically from a failure to adequately understand the real truth about raising, preparing, and packaging food.

Living organisms capture energy for their own use. Basically, all life on earth depends on the simple but powerful efforts of plants and algae that trap the light energy of the sun. Once that energy is trapped in chemical bonds, then Life can use it in various ways. Those biological activities generally involve combining the energy with minerals and water to produce more valuable substances. The body then applies those substances in millions of ways:

- ❑ Build better structures.
- ❑ Design and implement communication systems.
- ❑ Protect and defend the organism.
- ❑ Reproduce, and in doing so create a future for the species.
- ❑ The body even uses these energies and substances to help recycle itself when its time of living has passed.

Your pet's body needs a steady stream of highly nutritious foods to create maximum health. Ideally these foods are not laden with hidden toxins and are easily digested. The body will make do with all sorts of rotten, poor quality foods, but the worse the food quality, the more energy the body must expend to handle the food. Some foods take more energy to digest and eliminate than they provide to the body. Table 5.1 introduces some basic nutritional terms.

Nutritional Term	Definition
Calories	These represent the amount of energy provided by the food. The body needs calories (energy) to do work. Insufficient calories result in exhaustion. Excess calories result in obesity.
Calcium	This mineral is important to structure and function. Muscles and nerves won't function without correct calcium levels, and bones need calcium for strength and growth.
Fat	Fat is long chains of fatty acids. Good fat is needed for nerves, hormones, and cell structures (membranes).
Nutrients	Nutrients are components in food that are used by the body to improve its survival potential.
Proteins	Proteins, the basic building blocks, are made of amino acids assembled in chains. They are used to produce structures, hormones, and all important enzymes.
Carbohydrates	Starches such as rice, potatoes, pasta, corn, and wheat are carbohydrates, which are sources of energy for the body. They are made up of carbon and water. When they burn they release energy, carbon dioxide, and water. Excess carbohydrates are turned into fat.
Minerals	These are inorganic materials that provide structure and stability as well as electrical flows used by muscles and nerves.
Trace minerals	Trace minerals are those that the body uses in very small amounts. Excess amounts can be toxic, and insufficient amounts can cripple the immune system.
Preservatives	Chemicals that block enzymes and prevent food spoilage are called preservatives. They are needed in processed foods, but may damage your pet's delicate intestinal balance and more energy may need to be expended to properly digest and process these agents. When possible we prefer natural preservatives such as vitamin C, vitamin E, and essential oils such as rosemary oil.
Vitamins	Vitamins are chemicals produced by the body or ingested that assist in the chemical reactions needed for life processes. Many vitamins are antioxidants, which means they eat up or recycle free radicals that can harm normal cell structures.

Table 5.1. Some basic nutrients and their functions. Food consists of more than just fuel. Many nutrients are important to the body's continued survival for many reasons.

Our cats and dogs are carnivores. They eat body parts from other animals. They also eat fresh raw plant material and digested plant material from the stomachs of plant-eating animals that they kill or find dead. They consume flesh, bones, skin, and hair. Sometimes they eat body organs and other times they do not. Raw food is the food of choice for wild meat-eating animals. Raw meat actually assists in its own digestion because of the specialized proteins called enzymes, which occur in meat. The meat itself contains digestive enzymes and bacteria that make it easier for the hunter to digest and use its prey once the chase is over and the prey is caught and killed.

Modern scientific studies are just now learning about the incredible miracles of plant-based chemicals called "phytochemicals." It is likely that similar unknown or unevaluated compounds also exist in raw meaty foods. These "critter-chemicals" may have important effects on maintaining the health of our animals. Remember that modern "scientific" nutrition doesn't know about all the needs of normal bodies for these compounds (because they don't even know if and what they are, in many cases). However, we know that we see increased vitality and health, and even reversal of chronic diseases in many cases, if we provide dogs and cats with small amounts of these important substances. The table below shows some known phytochemicals. Realize that our scientific knowledge of these compounds is primitive at best. Note also that some phytochemicals are found in animals because they ingest them from plants, and so sometimes we can get phytochemicals from ingesting animal products as well as plants.

Phytochemical	Source	Actions/Uses
Cyanidin	Red fruits and veggies	Strong antioxidant, free radical scavenger, antitoxin mycotoxins; may help prevent diabetes
Lycopene	Veggies (tomatoes)	Anticancer, antibacterial, antifungal; protects diabetics against cardiovascular disease
Quercitin	Apples, tea, onions, nuts, berries, cauliflower, cabbage	Anticancer, antigout, reduces allergy symptoms; provides respiratory support
Resveratrol	Many plants, fruits, seeds	Antitoxic agent, anticancer, antioxidant; contributes to heart health; may slow aging changes
Coumarin	Several plants including sweet clover, strawberries, apricots, cherries, cinnamon, lavender, tonka beans	Antitumor, antifungal, blood thinning qualities
Silibinin	Milk thistle	Assists liver function and reduces damage from toxins
Hydroxytyrosol	Olives	Powerful antioxidant, anticancer; reduces damage from tobacco smoke; reduces hardening of the arteries in humans
Astaxanthin	Red crustaceans, microalgae	Antioxidant, free radical scavenger, provides immune system and mitochondrial support
Beta-Sitosterol	Plant-based diet, soy, corn oil, flaxseed, pumpkin seeds	Antioxidant, anticancer; supports prostate, lowers cholesterol

Table 5.2. Some common phytochemicals. Plants contain many chemicals that support bodily functions but are not known or fully studied. Such agents may contribute powerfully to the medical value of particular foods. Plants create phytochemicals but animals may contain them as we see with astaxanthin above, which is produced by microalgae that are consumed by crustaceans.

In veterinary school I was taught that commercial foods were the pinnacle of development in animal nutrition. I was taught that they contain everything a pet needs to stay healthy and that all professionals need to do is convince their clients to feed these premium foods and there would be no need to worry about nutrition.

That is not totally true.

It is true that pet food companies continue to improve their diets, but processed food is not fresh food, no matter how hard we try.

While cooking improves the safety of commercially available foods by killing parasites and pathogenic bacteria that can make animals sick, cooking or processing by any means changes the nutritional value of food. Cooking can increase the usefulness of certain nutrients and damage others. Commercially prepared food must be cooked at temperatures high enough to kill bacteria, and this means that important digestive enzymes are totally destroyed, which makes the body work harder to digest its food. The pancreas must supply many more digestive enzymes on a continuous basis when the entire diet is cooked. That can lead to exhaustion of organs such as the pancreas, and exhausted pancreases are more prone to develop diseases such as pancreatic inflammation and diabetes. Because pancreatic enzymes are used to both digest food and protect the body against tumors and toxin accumulation, this can leave the body with an inadequate amount of digestive enzymes to maintain good health. Some people feel that some forms of arthritis are a cooked-food disease, and in some cases we see improvement in joint pain in human and veterinary patients that are placed on whole food, unprocessed, raw diets.

Scientists recently have discovered that cooking has some desirable effects as well. Some nutrients actually improve with gentle cooking, so as scientific knowledge advances we may learn when to feed raw foods and when to cook certain foods, depending upon the patient's genetic makeup and the disease processes we are dealing with at a specific time. So it is not as simple as "cooked food is bad and raw food is good," and thoughtful animal stewards must work with their veterinarians to determine what feeding patterns are best for their pets.

Food can be negatively affected by cooking, but that is not the only way that foods are damaged after they are produced. Along with sitting in storage conditions at higher heat, which can damage the fat contained in diets, a new threat looms on the horizon. Recently governments in some countries such as Australia began requiring that packaged foods be treated with radiation before allowing their importation. A large number of cats became ill after consuming the irradiated diet. Consumers had no warning that the food they were buying was irradiated. It appears that radiation affects the food in some way that leads to neurological disease in cats. I am very suspicious of irradiated foods. While science insists that these foods are safe, I believe that irradiation alters the energetic quality of foods and may have subtle effects on health that we have yet to fully appreciate. These Australian cats may be sending us a warning and I hope we hear them. It should be a legal requirement that irradiated foods be properly labeled so consumers can make informed decisions.

Table 5.3 below shows some comparisons between cooked and raw foods.

Food Type	Protein* (g/100g)	Total Fat (g100g)	Vitamin A (IU/100g)	Vitamin C (mg/100g)	Vitamin E (mg/100g)	Beta Carotene (mcg/100g)	Lutein (mg/100g)
Raw chicken leg meat	18.15	12.12	123	2.5	0.44	0	0
Roasted chicken leg meat	27.03	8.43	63	0	0.27	0	0
Stewed chicken leg meat	26.26	8.06	60	0	0.27	0	0
Raw beef	20.64	9.51	0	0	0.33	0	0
Roasted beef	26.54	14.86	0	0	0.18	0	0
Raw spinach	2.86	0.39	9,377	28.1	2.03	5,626	12,198
Frozen cooked spinach	4.01	0.87	12,061	2.2	3.54	7,237	15,690
Canned cooked spinach	2.81	0.50	9,801	14.3	1.94	5,881	10,575
Raw kale	3.3	0.70	15,376	120	0	9,226	39,950
Cooked kale	1.9	0.40	13,621	41	0.85	8,173	18,246

Table 5.3. A comparison between raw and cooked foods. (Source: USDA National Nutrient Database for Standard Referencehttp://ultimatenutritiontables.com)
*When comparing cooked and raw foods and their percentage of protein, remember that cooking removes water and therefore makes the protein percentage higher. This does not mean that the food has more protein.

Detoxification

Our bodies take the food we eat and the fluids we drink, extract the useful components, and attempt to excrete the waste or unusable materials. Healthy compounds in food actually help the body excrete toxins and reduce the damage done by toxins in the body. When toxins have been ingested or when the food cannot be properly utilized, sometimes the body can't excrete a toxin properly, and so it ends up storing it in the body. Such accumulation and storage of toxins marks the beginning stages of chronic disease states.

Toxins are commonly stored in the fat and other types of connective tissue. Once toxic material is stored there, it can be dangerous for the body to remove the material because it can release waste products that can harm the body. This is a common reason why obese people cannot mobilize fat or lose weight. Many patients find that losing weight becomes easier after detoxification therapy. In fact, patients that simply could not lose weight often find their weight melting away after completing a course of detoxification. As the toxic material is safely removed and eliminated the body naturally wants to clear excessive fatty deposits, because they are unhealthy.

Fresh green veggies provide the liver and intestinal system with excellent support and detoxification powers. New studies prove that green vegetables actually activate the liver's natural detoxification system. They also turn off the switch that turns on liver cancer in people. Now, that is medicine we can all use and afford. Pharmaceutical companies are madly trying to isolate the specific ingredient or ingredients in green veggies so they can patent them and sell them for treatment of liver cancer, but why wait for the tumor or the expensive drug? Why not just eat more of these foods now?

Plants contain many necessary components that work synergistically to assist our bodies in creating a healthier environment. The fiber in vegetables binds toxins and carries them out of the gastrointestinal system. It stimulates the liver and gall bladder and makes the bowel work better. Veggies help the natural bacteria in the bowel to become healthier. The vitamins and minerals in fruits and green vegetables directly assist the body with construction, repair, and excretion functions.

Fresh green foods are high in minerals such as magnesium, potassium, sodium, and trace minerals that are so important to the proper functioning of many body elements. Muscles and nerves can't properly function without them, and our bodies cannot properly make energy without minerals. And remember that mineral content is higher in organically raised vegetables because organic farmers use richer soils that contain more minerals for the plants to absorb and process. Vitamins and enzymes are most active and easily absorbed by the body when these foods are eaten raw.

If you look further at table 5.3 there are several important things to observe and note:

1. Cooking greatly decreases levels of vitamins such as A, C, and E, which are vital in defending the body and its cells against attack by oxidation.
2. Cooking may damage certain plant antioxidants. Because there are literally thousands of chemicals in plants that scientists have yet to identify, it is reasonable to assume that cooking robs food of many other important but unknown nutrients.
3. Nutrition tables do not contain information about enzyme levels and activity. It is important to realize that cooking destroys all enzyme content, making enzymes inactive and useless in the digestive process. That means your pet's body must make more enzymes to digest processed, cooked, or chemically preserved foods.
4. While many people have been falsely taught that fat in the diet is bad, in actuality it is an important nutrient for predators. Without proper amounts of the right fats, our cell membranes develop holes that can let toxins in more easily. Cats desperately need adequate amounts of high quality animal fats in their diets for proper health. This is why they love to steal butter if you leave it out. Cooking decreases

fat levels and damages the delicate fats, making them less useful and in some cases even toxic. Fat-soluble vitamins (vitamin A) can be lost in cooking, as we see when we compare values for chicken.

5. The water is removed when food is cooked, which makes food dense and potentially harder to digest. It also makes it appear in tables such as these that the percentage of nutrients is higher, which is not actually the case.

6. Darker green, leafy vegetables contain massive amounts of nutrients and make excellent supplemental foods for people and pets, especially those who are chronically ill and need the higher levels of antioxidants and vitamins that these vegetables contain. Kale is a miracle veggie from this standpoint, but excess amounts can promote kidney stones, so use it in moderation (as with all foods).

7. Science has yet to identify most of the important therapeutic compounds in foods. And food scientists have barely even scraped the surface of understanding how individual ingredients in food work synergistically to help the body do its work. Nutrition tables list only the items we currently know about. That means that by simply comparing levels of simple vitamins and minerals we are probably missing many important and potentially therapeutic nutrients that simply have not been discovered, researched, and understood at this time. Scientific knowledge about nutrition is always far behind the organisms that create and manage Life. Science will never know as much as Mother Nature does, and so it is wise to eat a wide variety of foods in the most natural state possible.

8. Soil conditions greatly vary the nutritional analysis of foods, so 100 grams of spinach raised in a hydroponic farm vary greatly from 100 grams of spinach raised organically. This isn't even considering the potentially harmful chemical and pesticide levels,

which is another critical factor in feeding our pets. Therefore, we should always try to feed and eat the most naturally produced and minimally processed foods possible.

9. Storage of foods can damage their content. If mold grows on a crop, it can release very toxic compounds into the food. While normal quality control methods used by farmers and food producers minimize this issue, it is a good idea to eat food as fresh as possible. Eating fresh ingredients, obtained locally, allows a consumer more freedom to directly view the ingredients for acceptability. Processing allows for contaminated goods to be blended in without our direct ability to see that a particular food product is damaged or potentially unacceptable.

10. There is a reason that fresh, local, seasonal foods often taste better to us. Trust your senses and trust your pet's sense of taste and smell as well. They may sense things that you are unaware of and avoid foods that are not good for them. In a recent food contamination incident, many people reported that their cats did not like the melamine-contaminated foods and ate them only after objecting. Some of these clients expressed regret for not listening to their pets regarding this fact. Please note that not all rejections mean a food is bad or dangerous. But in most instances there is little reason to force a pet to eat something that it doesn't want. Trust in their wisdom too. Just like people, our pets have food preferences and they are not always healthy choices. Good stewardship requires that we pay attention and evaluate these factors when making food choices.

Keys to a Healthy Diet

Good food is a critical factor for creating and maintaining good health. It is just as essential as air and water to your pet living a healthy and long life. Because science's understanding of good nutrition and health is incomplete, how do we ensure that our pets receive the best foods possible?

Remember that just because something can be eaten does not make it a nutrient. Junk may taste good but it isn't really food. Food is something that helps the body grow and repair. The following simple, common sense feeding rules can be used by anyone:

1. Fresh food is better than old food unless we are talking about naturally fermented foods such as yogurt. The older a food is, and the more it is processed from its natural state, the less nutritious and the greater the possibility that it contains harmful compounds such as rancid fatty acids, which increase chances of inflammatory diseases and even cancer. Fresh veggies, meats, and fruits contain substances that are more easily absorbed and active in protecting the body from disease and aging. Fresh foods and herbs contain many compounds that complement the positive effects and minimize the harmful effects of other components.

2. If it smells really bad, it likely isn't good food. Your nose, and that of your pet, has a purpose and ability that has evolved over millions of years. The nervous system is repelled by unhealthy smells and we should pay attention to this. Open a bag of processed, preserved "meat" treats and chances are that you are not excited about tasting these things. That is because they require lots of energy and work for the body's digestive and immune systems. Some of these things are even toxic and harmful.

3. Because the body developed by eating real food, it is naturally better to feed it real food than junk, and then try to correct that issue by adding chemical supplements.

4. The more non-nutritious chemicals that are added to a food, the greater the opportunities for them to cause digestive upsets or health challenges.

5. Choosing diets that are nutritionally complete and balanced is advised for our pets to live longer, better lives. This is something that science does know about diet and nutrition.

6. Feed a variety of commercial and fresh foods to give pets the best chance of eating a diet that is complete and balanced for their needs. This is the safest bet, since science doesn't know everything there is to know about nutrition.

7. Feeding easily digested, properly balanced diets allows for adequate calories as well as nutrition density (lots of vitamins, minerals, and phytochemicals). Providing higher-protein, nutrition-dense foods with normal levels of high quality fat and bioavailable minerals helps fight obesity because the body takes what it needs without having to eat massive amounts of grains or other fillers. This assumes that your pet has proper digestive processes in place (in many pets digestion must be addressed as part of their therapy).

8. Fiber in the proper amount is good. Too much or too little is bad for your pet.

9. Preservatives block enzymes and prevent food from rotting. That can also negatively affect digestion and healthy bacteria in the gut, particularly in those who are more sensitive. Fresh foods have no preservatives and contain healthy bacteria that assist digestion and immunity. They also assist in detoxification of chemical additives in commercially prepared foods. Select a diet with minimal preservatives and keep it well protected from humidity, heat, and room air. Keeping the food tightly sealed helps prevent oxidative damage and spoiling. Don't buy too much food at a time because it can get stale. It

is obviously faster to buy fresh food than wait in your veterinarian's waiting room with a sick pet.

10. Feed a diet that agrees with your pet. Good food leads to vitality, bright eyes, and a shiny coat. No single food or recipe will do this for all dogs or cats, and so as animal stewards we need to work with our pets to find the diet that serves them best. Furthermore, we need to realize that their dietary needs change markedly with age and specific health challenges. Your veterinarian should be a source of helpful information on nutrition. Ask for help and encourage your veterinarian to learn both traditional and complementary veterinary nutrition, so he or she is comfortable discussing a wide variety of topics on nutrition.

11. Feeding a good quality "holistic" commercial diet mixed with 20 percent to 30 percent high quality fresh food is an easy way to feed most pets. The owner who is really interested in pursuing raw food feeding must carefully follow a satisfactory recipe and not change it too much. Not all pets do well on raw diets, but many do extremely well on properly prepared raw foods.

Commercial pet foods can be fed, and many of my patients eat healthy diets that consist of high quality processed foods. There are many quality products available now. Not everyone has the time to prepare food for their pets, but most people can include *some* raw or lightly processed foods in their pets' diet, and this is generally a good thing. A simple way to support pets fed commercial foods involves making a supplemental diet. This can be made in larger batches and frozen in individual servings, which can be thawed and fed daily.

The following is the very simple "purification diet" recipe for dogs (consult with your veterinarian before using any treatment to be sure that it is appropriate for your pet):

Some of my favorite commercial diets include: Innova, Innova EVO, Pinnacle, Mereck, Organics, and Before Grain.

- 40 percent meat (If bones are included be sure they are finely ground. Also, see the cautions below for raw meat; do not use bones or skin in cooked or partially cooked meat unless advised by your veterinarian.)
- 30 percent carbohydrate (rice, potato, sweet potato, pasta); avoid wheat in allergic patients
- 30 percent veggies (green beans, carrots, asparagus, broccoli, kale, collard greens, romaine lettuce, Brussels sprouts, alfalfa sprouts, mung bean sprouts, etc.)
- Cook meat lightly and reserve the fat. Cook grains or carbohydrates and cube or mash. Lightly steam veggies or feed raw if your pet's digestive system can handle this without gas or other upset. Cut veggies into smaller pieces because dogs don't chew their food and fresh veggies need to be in small enough particles to help the digestive process. When using veggies and fruits be careful of diarrhea. If your dog gets gas or loose stools, then cut down the fruit and veggies and go a bit slower to give their digestive tract time to adapt to the new diet. Keep this recipe simple in the beginning and gradually add foods to see which best suit your dog. Blueberries pack

a punch of antioxidant nutrition and many dogs accept bananas, as well.

- Avoid garlic, onions, nuts, avocadoes, grapes, raisins, and chocolate unless you have specific instructions from your veterinarian. Garlic and onions can damage red blood cell membranes and must be used with caution. Some nuts (macadamia) are toxic to dogs. Grapes and raisins can cause irreversible, fatal kidney failure in some dogs, and should never be given to dogs under any circumstances. Other veggies such as broccoli can make pets sick if they are fed in excess, so keep amounts reasonable. If your pet has a negative reaction to a food it is best to record this on a calendar and discuss this with your pet's veterinarian before continuing to feed it.
- Organic produce has more nutrients per pound than commercially raised veggies and fruits. You don't have to feed organic produce, because any fresh food is better than no fresh food, but organic is better when it is available and affordable.
- Feed this diet three times weekly, along with your commercial diet, so it comprises about 20 percent to 30 percent of your pet's intake. It can be fed exclusively for two to four weeks if your dog is ill or needs pepping up.
- **Please note**: This diet does not contain adequate calcium and may be lacking in proper nutritional balance; therefore it is NOT for feeding long term as the exclusive diet. For long-term feeding it is best to consult with a board certified veterinary nutritionist. A simple way to do this is through the Balance It Web site: www.balanceit.com. I also recommend a holistically inclined veterinary nutritionist such as Dr. Susan Wynn (http://www.susanwynn.com).

Raw Food Diets

Raw food diets are popular with consumers, and many holistic doctors often use them. However, they may cause certain problems, and care is needed when electing to feed raw diets. Raw meat can spread parasitic disease such as toxoplasmosis. Raw food diets can also increase shedding of dangerous bacteria, such as *Salmonella*, from your pet's stool, which presents a risk to immunocompromised people. Bone fragments in raw food can lacerate and damage the bowel and even result in the need for surgery. The largest risk in feeding raw food diets is that most are not complete and balanced, and the resulting incomplete nutrition may lead to serious diseases such as rickets. Even when consumers are given complete and balanced recipes there is a tendency to alter the recipe over time; therefore, the diets can become incomplete due to owner noncompliance. There is increasing pressure on doctors not to recommend raw food diets. Some attorneys are threatening lawsuits against veterinarians who recommend these diets due to these risks, which can be substantial.

In spite of these issues, many clients make an informed decision to use simple raw diets such as Feline Instincts or My Natural Canine (www.felineinstincts.com). They can be fed exclusively or combined with high quality commercial diets. These diets are easy to prepare and cost effective. Because you buy your own fresh meat and mix it with the prepared supplement purchased from the company, consumers are better protected from dietary adulteration and contamination. Good pet stores often carry a variety of frozen raw foods, which also make this process easier. Prairie and Bravo are good selections, but no company is safe from contamination issues. Always use caution, and if your pet becomes ill following ingestion of any food, it is best to discontinue feeding that food, report the situation to the diet's manufacturer, and seek veterinary advice. Illness linked to foods should be reported by you or your veterinarian to the appropriate public health care organizations. Consumers and veterinarians can report suspect pet food contamination to the FDA at: http://www.vin.com/

WebLink.plx?URL=http://www.fda.gov/AnimalVeterinary/
SafetyHealth/ReportaProblem/ucm182403.htm.

I strongly recommend that pet owners consult with their veterinarians and even with a veterinary nutritionist about selecting the best dietary strategy for their individual pets because no diet suits all pets and all stages of life. Raw food is definitely not appropriate for all veterinary patients.

Vitamins
Many people do not realize that chemically synthesized vitamins often do not contain all the parts of naturally oc-curring vitamins. Or they contain chemical forms that are not easily used by the body's naturally existing enzyme systems.

For example, most people think that vitamin C is ascor-bic acid. Nutritional textbooks usually state this—some even call it a fact—but this is not true. Synthetic vitamin C, which is misleadingly called ascorbic acid, is made from sugar that has been altered into ascorbic acid. Naturally occur-ring vitamin C contains ascorbic acid, which helps protect the integrity of the whole vitamin, but it also contains sev-eral other important components that are necessary for its proper functioning. Synthetic ascorbic acid actually works more like a drug in the body than the natural vitamin, and this explains why people need to take such high doses to get benefits from synthetic vitamin C supplements.

A similar situation occurs with vitamin E. Natural vitamin E has several biologically active compounds. One com-ponent of vitamin E, E-2, is a powerful protector of heart function and can be used to control pain in angina. Very small doses of these naturally occurring vitamins may do more than very large doses of the synthetic ones. The body evolved using these substances and prefers naturally oc-curring vitamins as well as naturally occurring foods.

Although synthetic vitamins are certainly safer than many drugs, they can act like drugs and we see more toxicity and adverse reactions from their use, so pet owners should be aware that they can harm pets' delicate balance. Sometimes giving large doses of synthetic vitamins makes a pet appear to feel better, and this may be an important step in treating some medical conditions. However, vitamins used this way create their effects by stimulating or suppressing natural systems. Furthermore, providing massive levels of some vitamins requires the body to waste energy to excrete excessive amounts.

These vitamins also can accumulate and damage organs such as the liver. As a clinician, I use synthetic vitamins for certain conditions, but for most healthy pets, I don't advise additional supplementation with synthetics. When we do use synthetic vitamins (such as for arthritis and cancer patients) we recognize that we are using them more as drugs than as nutrition supplements and this helps such patients live better, happier, longer, and more pain-free lives.

The best way to meet your pet's nutritional needs is to feed a well-balanced diet with fresh ingredients. Proper nutrition provides the needed building blocks in the form nature intended for growth, regeneration, and repair. Feeding foods that are less processed, organically raised, and fresh actually provides the body with direct defense against toxins and disease-causing organisms and can even destroy cancer cells before they take hold.

> *Seeking and applying correct nutritional information may be the most powerful preventive medicine available to pet owners.*

✳ ✳ ✳

Part 2.
Disease and Healing

"Everyone has a doctor in him
or her; we just have to help it
in its work. The natural healing
force within each one of us is
the greatest force in getting
well. Our food should be
our medicine. Our medicine
should be our food."

Hippocrates (460 BC–377 BC)

Chapter 6. How Your Pet's Body Becomes Susceptible to Disease

Creating Health

If your pet's body has developed for maximal survival and has such amazing reparative capabilities, why and how does illness take root, and why are we seeing rising death rates from chronic diseases such as organ failure and cancer? There are many answers to this question and all of them have some value in understanding ways to improve the health and well-being of veterinary patients.

I have a vested interest in getting these answers because there are simply too many sick animals in this world. I work hard caring for the sixteen thousand pets that come to our practice each year and it is nearly impossible to run an appointment schedule that is constantly interrupted by emergency visits. I long for the day when people actively create health and I dream of the day when we see fewer chronically ill pets. Our practice has seen increased life expectancies since including complementary and holistic modalities in our patients' treatment plans, and we are working to include still more holistic methods of improving health and delaying the onset of disease. I've cooperated with other integrative doctors to help spread the word and teach other professionals about these techniques. Each author of our textbook, *Integrating Complementary Medicine into Veterinary Practice*, came to the project in hopes of helping people and pets get healthy and stay healthy. It is a major dream of all good veterinarians, whether they are integrative or conventional.

No sane person likes to see sick animals.

No one likes premature illness and death.

That is why we are communicating through this book right now.

So, how does illness get started?

The body's immune system is awe inspiring. If it is intact, or one might say, "well integrated" (integration means intact and whole), it readily recognizes threats and responds to them. From that simple statement we can start to understand where the system can break down. We call things that stress the body and predispose it to illness a simple term known as "stressors." There are many possible stressors, but they tend to break down into seven categories:

1. Nutritional problems (deficiencies; excesses; imbalances; and troubles with digestion, absorption or elimination of food, and digestive wastes)
2. Immune challenges (bacteria, fungi, viral, and other disease-causing organisms)
3. Parasites (fleas, mites, worms, protozoa, and other organisms that steal energy and substance from the body)
4. Chemical poisoning (toxicity from chemicals, heavy metals, drugs, etc.)
5. Scars (addressed below)
6. Psychical stress (including emotional, mental, or spiritual upset)
7. Genetic errors

The body operates as a system in balance. Anything that upsets that balance demands a response, or imbalance occurs. Prolonged imbalance leads to distress and disease. Because Life involves constantly responding to changing conditions, an organism and its friends and allies must constantly respond to Life in ways that maximize survival and minimize harm. In its highest sense this occurs when the organism has access to correct information and can evaluate and use that information properly to act effectively at a microscopic and macroscopic level. The summation of all these survival efforts by the organism result in the present "condition" of the pet.

> If we add up everything that is right about our pet and then subtract what is wrong, we get the overall condition of our pet's body. That is its health quotient, or HQ.

In other words, if we add up everything that is right about an organism and then subtract what is wrong, we get the overall condition of our pet's body. That is its health quotient, or HQ. We can't really calculate such a number, but it is a handy concept to keep in mind. Your HQ would reflect your precise medical condition at any moment.

As we learned before, that word "condition" is an important one. While we have lost this sense of the word in modern language, it means precisely "what has been agreed with." So if we agree with things that subject the body to the chronic stressors listed above, we increase the chances for disease to occur. If we take a body in healthy condition and then subject it to chronic stressors while not providing it with what is needed to recover and heal, then we take it from a condition of health and ease to a state of DIS-EASE. Disease is a condition wherein the body has lost its integrity and ability to handle its normal functions.

Seven Stressors

The medicine of the future must learn to address these seven stressors if we are to evolve better care for our patients. They are:

1. Nutritional imbalance
2. Immune challenges
3. Parasites
4. Chemical poisoning
5. Scars
6. Psychical stress
7. Faulty genetics

Another word I like is "consequence," which means "the order of things that occur from a cause." Look for a moment at the consequences in the following scenario: Humankind fails to properly care for the land. Topsoil and the nutrients it contains erode and are not replaced. Farmers raise foods that look good but are deficient in minerals and nutrition. Company AYZ makes food for your pet from these foods and processes out even more nutrition. After eating such food for several years, the lack of nutrients leads to a reduced ability to detoxify and repair the body, and obesity, heart disease, diabetes, and arthritis develop. You arrive at your veterinarian wondering why your bills are so high and why your pet needs so many drugs just to live.

It takes an increased sense of personal responsibility to view this situation, but it helps a responsible person understand and then act in ways to improve the situation. That is really what this chapter is about—doing what we can to improve health and well-being and to assist pets that are sick in repairing and reversing at least some of their disease processes.

Reducing the effects of those seven stressors is a key to this effort. Look at the list of seven stressors again. Now let's examine how we can take a puppy and approach this process very simply. Genetics is an issue that comes to us when we get a new pet, and while it is last on the list, it actually precedes the arrival of the puppy into your home and affects its condition for its entire life.

Your new puppy arrives and at this moment the two of you begin a lifelong journey. Decisions and choices you make in these formative years will affect you both for many years. Obviously you want to provide your new puppy with a safe space with plenty of good food and fresh water and minimal psychical stressors. This allows it to have what it needs to become interested and grow properly and safely. If we provide interesting play and proper conditions, then the genetic potential of the pet can be maximally expressed. Genetics provide your pet's maximum potential. The environment you provide allows them to manifest that potential.

We all know that understanding situations and knowing how to respond reduces stress. Imagine being hired for a new job and then being told to go to work with no instruction or introductions. You'd be a basket case pretty quickly. This is true for our pets as well. Properly training pets leads to reduced stress and increased happiness and is a part of the process of helping your pet reach its maximum potential. Training helps to establish the communication and control systems of both puppy and caregiver. Making this a positive, win-win experience is really important because it allows the puppy's nervous system to properly develop and prevents excessive amounts of stress hormones that can interfere with immune function and proper growth.

In the confines of a safe environment, good nutrition becomes the most important issue. Properly fed pets are very hard to make ill. Their strong vitality coupled with their excellent diet protects them against all sorts of diseases. Good nutrition helps them defend themselves against the other stressors. Hopefully, by now you see the magnitude and real importance of proper nutrition.

Feeding puppies (and kittens) a good quality commercial diet designed for them is important because they have higher demands for phosphorus, calcium, and protein than adult pets and they have much higher energy needs. They grow quickly and need good building blocks to do this optimally, but excess nutrition is undesirable. Making a baby overweight condemns it to a life of obesity and weight-related health issues, so feed your puppy or kitten so that it stays in lean body condition. You can assess this by simply feeling under your pet's armpits. A lean pet should have readily palpable ribs under its elbows. If you feel fat, your puppy or kitten is likely overweight. Your veterinarian can help you determine this as part of the first visits, and you should regularly monitor this for maximal health potential.

Early Susceptibility

For the first few weeks your pet should be kept strictly at home in a safe space that is free of contagious diseases. Infectious viruses and parasites often contaminate parks, beaches, and streets. Please be aware that some of these viruses are in the soil and can come into your home on the soles of your shoes. Removing your shoes upon entering the home can reduce the chances of viral infections gaining access to your new pet. This is particularly important in preventing canine parvovirus, a severe form of vomiting and diarrhea in dogs.

Feeding a proper diet designed for growth assists in immune system growth and development, but it takes time for this to happen. In our office we often recommend using a whole food supplement to support the pet's immune system during growth and vaccination challenges that occur during puppy and (kitten) hood. Your veterinarian can make this recommendation on your first puppy or kitten wellness examination.

Certain diseases such as feline distemper and canine parvovirus easily infect newborns and often result in death without aggressive treatment. In the beginning, you can protect your puppy from canine parvovirus by keeping it isolated, but eventually it begins to grow up and, as it seeks larger areas, the need to protect against other diseases increases.

This is where vaccines and regular deworming enter, and where your veterinarian is well equipped to assist you and your puppy. A later chapter addresses vaccine issues; simply know that vaccines save lives, but they need to be properly and appropriately administered because they can also create stress and disease in certain pets. Vaccines help the immune system learn how to survive attack by dangerous viruses and bacteria, but they also can contain chemical toxins and live virus particles, which can become trapped in the body and lead to other disease syndromes. Their use deserves proper respect and care by veterinarians and pet owners alike. This is a topic that pet owners must discuss openly with their veterinarian before proceeding.

While vaccines, like proper nutrition, assist the body in defending against intruders, it is neither possible nor desirable to vaccinate for every possible virus and bacteria. Your pet can gain exposure to common diseases and learn how to defend against them simply by gradually being introduced to an increasing sphere of contact in the world. In a pet that is properly fed, this process occurs naturally and with a minimum of difficulty.

Parasites

Seventy percent of all puppies are infected with parasitic round worms, also called ascarids. The mother's milk contains tiny parasitic larvae that transfer to the puppy. This happens in kittens too. These parasites can make the puppy or kitten ill with diarrhea, or they can simply eat the animal's food and suppress local immunity in the intestinal tract. They also migrate and damage organs. Most owners are unaware that their new puppy or kitten is harboring these nasty worms because they live in the small intestine and don't pass out in the stool. However, their microscopic eggs and larvae pass out in the stool and can infect people. Regular deworming can reduce the damage caused by parasites and every puppy or kitten should be dewormed regularly and checked for parasites.

We recommend the first deworming at two weeks of age in puppies and kittens. This should be repeated every two to three weeks until the pet is sixteen weeks old. Be sure to carefully clean up all pet waste and instruct children in the area to wash their hands after handling animals, because these parasites are microscopic and can transfer to dirty hands. Fingers in the mouth lead to accidental ingestion of parasites and then health issues, so proper hygiene and regular parasite treatment is the best way to avoid this stressor.

All puppies and kittens should continue to receive proper parasite control at regular intervals. It is usually not advisable to use more toxic and potentially dangerous herbal dewormers in our pets because modern parasite control methods work so well and are so gentle.

Flea control is necessary in much of the country. Some pets have trouble with certain flea control products; if that's the case you and your veterinarian can cooperate and design a specific program that is best for your area and climate.

Toxic Chemicals and Water

Avoiding toxic chemicals is not always possible, but often our decisions affect our pets' health. Smoking is a perfect example. Most people know that smoking increases lung diseases such as cancer, and most are aware of second-hand smoke, but did you know that cats living in smoking households have a fourteen times higher rate of lymphoid cancer? This doesn't come from inhaling the smoke, but from licking it off their fur. Smoke in the environment is drawn to hair and binds there. Cats groom their hair and swallow tobacco smoke, which contaminates their lymph system and causes intestinal cancer. Many of my clients stopped smoking when they learned this. I have seen people devastated when they learn that their smoking has caused their pets' cancer and the pets now require chemotherapy and long-term treatment.

Drugs can also be toxic chemicals; therefore, use of antibiotics, cortisone, and psychiatric and anti-inflammatory drugs should be kept to the absolute minimum. When they must be used, take appropriate steps afterward to repair the damage caused by their use. Anti-inflammatories and antibiotics directly harm the intestines and can damage kidney and liver tissue. Anti-inflammatory drugs are often given as pain medication, but owners must understand that they can decrease healing; often other pain management techniques are better for juvenile patients undergoing surgery. Psychiatric drugs can cause permanent changes to neural pathways, which may not be desirable. In humans they are associated with increased death rates in geriatric patients. In addition to causing vomiting and diarrhea, side effects that are annoying, some of these psychiatric drugs are associated with increased aggressive or unpredictable behavior. Always discuss the issues of potential adverse reactions with your veterinarian when your pet is prescribed medication.

Sometimes foods themselves are the source of toxins. Food additives are not always listed clearly as ingredients in a diet. Ingredients such as vegetable hydrozylates or acid digests may sound healthy, but are actually a source of monosodium glutamate (MSG), which is used to falsely stimulate increased ingestion of foods and may actually be neurotoxic. While these chemicals appear in small amounts, we are just learning about how they can combine with other chemicals and yield yet other chemicals that are harmful to the body's natural defenses. This concept is called synergism and is a very important idea that helps us understand why chemicals can cause so much difficulty and disease.

Water can be a common source of toxin ingestion, so it is essential to offer plenty of clean, fresh water to keep the immune system functioning. Unfortunately, toxic agents such as arsenic appear in many domestic water supplies, as do other chemicals such as fluoride, plastics, pesticides, chlorine, and chloramines. Recent testing of public water supplies found residues of more than fifty prescription drugs. Most domestic water supplies are not dangerous and simply purchasing a water filter that uses activated charcoal does much to reduce many of these toxins. Bottled water may not be better; it may be contaminated with plastic compounds that upset the system of some animals and people. Contact your local public health department or water utility company to obtain an analysis of your municipality's water supply.

Beware of private parties selling water quality testing. Recently one such laboratory told a client of mine that her tap water contained deadly amounts of lead. This client spent several thousand dollars handling the nonexistent situation only to find out that the lab's testing was faulty. Water is a needed commodity and clean water is a critical issue for us all, but there are people who make large amounts of money claiming that water in your home is not safe. Use discretion and carefully evaluate fear-based company claims before committing to buying these services.

A final note about water: Simply letting a pet become dehydrated, even slightly, changes the way its natural police officers function and greatly reduces the strength of the immune system. Furthermore, simple dehydration also makes it harder to excrete toxins from the body. Important research into aging has shown that relative dehydration of our connective tissues occurs as we age.

If you are interested in how chemicals can destroy health, I highly recommend the book *The Hundred Year Lie: How to Protect Yourself from the Chemicals That Are Destroying Your Health* by Randall Fitzgerald. It can be a bit depressing but it contains information that people really need to know to make the best health choices for themselves and their animals. It can be a very useful text if you use it as a source of information that you can act on.

Scars

Active scars are another very important stressor. While European doctors have known about and dealt with scars for many years, most doctors in the United States have no idea how harmful scars are to health. I think this information is vital to every single man, woman, and child in the world, and our pets need owners who understand how scars can harm health. A scar is a mix of connective tissue that follows damage to the body. The body's nervous system consists of a fine weblike network of nerves that cover every aspect of the body, something most people don't appreciate. This network conveys information about the body as well as instructions from the central control systems.

Anything that interferes with proper nerve function can act as a stressor and predispose one to a disease condition. Not all cuts or damage result in active scars, but scars can act like electrical storage devices called capacitors, storing energy and suddenly releasing it upon the nervous system. Scars on the bodies of patients (ear crops, spay and neuter, old fight wounds, etc.) can affect organ function. We have seen scars cause or worsen thyroid dysfunction and many other problems including behavioral aggression. Natural health practitioners frequently identify this problem in women who have had episiotomies and body jewelry. It is amazing to discover that major health issues can be treated by simply finding and treating one or more of these active scars. The simplest treatment involves rubbing pure wheat germ oil onto the scar daily for thirty days. We recommend this once surgery wounds have healed, especially after routine neutering surgery in male and female pets.

Coming Full Circle: Back To Genetics

Our discussion of stressors returns to genetics. Your new puppy comes to you with a certain genetic package of strengths and weaknesses. Good nutrition is known to protect genes and prevent activation of genetic conditions such as aging and cancer. Certain nutritional and homeo-pathic therapies might even reverse some genetic dam-age, but this is far from being completely understood. We know that purebred animals have more genetic problems because they have been raised in an abnormal genetic environment. Instead of selecting for important survival qualities, purebred breeders often select for traits that are actually harmful, such as malformed joints, malformed re-spiratory systems, hair coats that are too long or faulty, or defective immunity. Mixed-breed dogs tend to have fewer genetic defects and are stronger due to their mixed genet-ic heritage. This is called "hybrid vigor" and it results when broader pools of genetic possibilities are involved in the pet's heritage. Many people prefer to adopt mixed-breed pets because they tend to have fewer genetic issues.

I love pug dogs. They are fun and interesting, but the ge-netics that make up this breed are based upon fatal genes. If a wild dog delivers a puppy with the pug gene, she will refuse to feed it and let it die because she recognizes that the small airways, over-long soft palate, misplaced and mis-aligned teeth, and abnormal skeleton are not good qualities for a predator to posses. People likes these dogs, but we have damaged their genetics in creating this breed. Boxer dogs, Persian cats, Chinese shar-peis, and golden retrievers have all been damaged to the point that they frequently develop genetic-based diseases and have high rates of cancer.

If we return to our discussion of conditions and conse-quences, we find that selecting one of these breeds means we are agreeing to more diseases than by selecting other choices. It is fine to select a breed known to have problems, but do not be surprised when those genetic issues surface and must be cared for. And anyone who chooses one of these breeds should learn which genetic diseases affect their particular breed so they can minimize the problems associated with these issues.

Viruses, chemical toxicities, and nutritional decisions can negatively affect genetics. A scientist named Dr. Francis M. Pottenger, Jr., demonstrated that he could readily document the decline of genetic health in cats by feeding processed food. He also demonstrated that genetic health could be positively reversed in these cats by correcting their diets. It took several generations, but this damage was repaired. Again, we return to the importance of nutrition and call it the single most important aspect of your pet's health that you can directly influence.

Mental and Spiritual Stress: Psychical Stressors

The area of psychical stressors can be a difficult one to discuss. People have many established or fixed ideas about this, but I would simply say that I believe that living Beings have awareness and work toward survival. I capitalize the word Being when I am referring to a sentient organism. I think that we are composite Beings that consist of a spiritual aspect, a mental aspect, and a physical aspect. I find awareness in sentient Beings that stems from spirit and manifests as mind and body. These components work together to ensure or improve the chances of survival for a particular organism. When something opposes that survival urge, it creates stress. If this goes unhandled the result is disease. This origination of disease can take many forms and is beyond the scope of this text, but suffice it to say that living with stress or constant unpredictable behavior lowers a pet's ability to stay healthy.

When we live, and when our pets live, we communicate and create actions in a wide sphere. The body needs action to heal. Action actually coordinates the healing intention with the purpose of the mind and body. Exercise, when done properly, reduces stress because it tells the body through physical use which repairs are needed. Energy flows through moving body parts and this assists in the transfer of toxic material and vital nutrients needed for repair and maintenance.

Activity aligns and coordinates growth with nutrition and immunity, and is critical for all stages of your pet's growth and development. Getting proper exercise for your pet helps both your lives, and is likely responsible for the improved health statistics of pet owners. We give pets a safe space and they make our lives richer for the relationship. And in living we create actions, and cooperation occurs. Coordination and cooperation are enjoyable things by themselves—isn't that what dancing is all about?

> Chronic, unhandled stress prevents a pet from properly digesting and handling its food, increases waste products, and reduces the body's ability to repair itself.

One final thought about stress: Stress occurs when there is a persistent threat to survival about which one perceives he can do little or nothing. It results when the spirit, mind, and body are misaligned or when the relationships of these three elements suffer disharmony. Stress is also a hormonal event in the body that results in larger amounts of cortisone being produced by the adrenal glands. This leads to a wide variety of problems that damage the immune system, harm the intestines and gut, and lead to a tendency toward obesity.

Wound healing is negatively affected by stress, and stressed Beings are more likely to become wounded. Punishment creates stress, but understanding (training) reduces stress. Constant inadequate or excess nutrition leads to stress; chemical toxicity leads to stress and predisposes to infections and tumors.

Stressors cause stress.

Stress leads to disease.

We see that by correctly identifying stress and responding to the actual issue at hand, we have the chance to reduce stress and create ease (not dis-ease) for the organism. Some misinterpret this to mean taking drugs and falling into some unaware stupor, which in actuality is a chemical toxicity that is incredibly stressful for the body. A stress-free space and world is not necessarily desirable or possible, but excessive, chronic, unhandled stress is definitely not beneficial.

We can support our pets emotionally by teaching them proper behavior and communication with good training techniques. We can help them handle their stressors by learning some simple yet important facts about them. You can see how these actions, coupled with everything else we have discussed, immensely helps to create healthier conditions.

Dr. Bert Brooks is a friend of mine and a member of the research committee of the American Holistic Veterinary

Medical Association. Dr. Brooks was the first to make me fully see how chronic diseases are often (if not always) the result of nutritional imbalance, chemical toxicity, and viral activity. In medicine we spend so much time and effort fighting and protecting against viruses, but we miss the critical steps that precede and lead to chronic diseases. The medicine, or more correctly, the civilization of the future, must learn to address these seven stressors if we are to evolve better care for our patients.

This chapter is dense with information. If your pet gets sick I recommend returning here and reviewing these seven stressors in an attempt to find out more about what is causing its lowered health. An integrative doctor, especially one skilled in muscle response testing, can really help in this area. As you make your daily observations, keep them in mind and you will find that you can make better decisions and help your pet's body recover from stress and disease. From a holistic viewpoint, if we live our lives by taking actions to minimize the stressors that we create in our activities, we are making a better world one decision at a time.

Stress is caused by "stressors." Unhandled stress causes disease. Find and properly handle the correct stressors and health can begin to re-emerge. That is the process necessary to achieving miracles and finding personal happiness. It is worth doing.

✵ ✵ ✵

Chapter 7. Introductory Guide to Integrative Practice

Medicine's Constant Evolution

The huge field of medicine must reflect all of Life, and as such must have the means to handle anything that involves Life. Our healing needs to reflect our lives, and our pets are no exception. Each generation faces different challenges, so it follows that medicine must remain flexible and should be careful of losing technology.

Lost medical technology may not be immediately noticed until a particular health challenge re-emerges and patients find a need for its use. Some forms of medical technology are as timeless as the basic system of Life present in each species. These "ancient" healing arts have traveled with us from their inception until the present time. There are undoubtedly other medical modalities that are not even properly conceived, let alone understood to the point that they are useful. This is a major challenge for medicine: Keep the technology intact while expanding its efficacy for the purpose of improving longevity and quality of life.

Medicine has lots to do with seeking and finding Truth and documenting it for all times. When Truth is found it becomes proven scientifically; we understand it with greater clarity and begin to use it with predictable results. This application of properly found and understood Truth gives rise to technology, and every great civilization is known by its technologies and how it uses them to serve others.

Truth, when found and properly identified, leads to increased rates of healing. A diagnosis that has no cure is a sure sign that there is more to discover and tools to be found to better help patients afflicted with a particular disease. There are many incurable disease conditions that draw investigators to better understand them.

This chapter discusses the basic points that anyone should know when working with healing arts. They help us understand and act effectively, and I use them daily in my practice.

Hering's Law of Cure

Constantine Hering was a famous American physician who, in the 1800s, was sent by the conventional doctors of the day to expose the father of homeopathy, Samuel Hahnemann, as a fraud. Hering, after working with Hahnemann, found him to be quite brilliant and ahead of his time in healing arts. He wrote that Hahnemann was doing true science and documenting illness and healing like no one had done before. Constantine Hering established the first homeopathic medical school in the United States in 1835, in Pennsylvania, where it remains today as an orthodox medical school: the Hahnemann Medical College and Hospital. Hering was a well-respected natural physician who published extensively. It is unfortunate that, of the many medicines introduced by Hering, only nitroglycerine, a homeopathic medicine commonly used in conventional cardiology, remains in medical practice as a tribute to his medical genius.

As Hering treated patients he observed that some of their signs of disease were followed by recovery, but others would worsen. He was interested in finding relationships and methods to determine when doctors should be pleased with patients' changing conditions and when they should become concerned and intervene. Hering's Law of Cure is really not a law, but rather an observation of how patients often responded when their own bodies were beginning to heal. It assists doctors and patients in recognizing healing when it is occurring so that they do not take actions that could halt the progress of this natural healing.

Hering's Law states:

1. The body repairs from inside to outside,
2. From most important organ to least important organ,
3. From the head down to extremities, and
4. In reverse order of the patient's present pathologic history. This means that symptoms of diseases the patient suffered from in the past can reappear as the body clears its connective tissues.

When we use natural therapies we frequently see this course of healing appear. If we know the rules, then we can choose better methods for our patients to heal. In my practice, many people seek us out for natural approaches to skin conditions and allergies. We have helped many pets with these difficult problems, but it is hard work for sure. Pets may have signs of illness such as itching or rashes that last for one to three years as they clear a myriad of illness factors.

Foxy: A Case Example of Hering's Law

Foxy was a three-year-old neutered bulldog. He had been plagued by unending skin infections for several years. If he stopped taking antibiotics, a skin infection would quickly appear. This infection usually involved his face, chin, and feet, and would eventually spread to the entire body. He had trouble year round, with no worsening during one season or another (seasonal skin problems are often allergic in nature). Foxy had seen many very competent veterinarians and he had been well tested in an attempt to find his problem. He had skin scrapings to look for parasites and blood tests to check his white blood cells and hormone levels. His skin had been cultured and his doctors had properly treated him with the right antibiotics at the right dosage and for adequate periods of time. He had been fed several different foods in an attempt to find any food allergy, but in each case the infection would resolve on antibiotics and then recur once the medicine was stopped.

I told Foxy's human mom about the difficulty of such cases. These dogs often have abnormal immune systems and do not always respond to treatment. I discussed Hering's Law of Cure and she agreed to potentially long and possibly expensive therapy with no guarantee of a cure. She said that she was glad to do this because nothing else had worked for Foxy and she loved him immensely.

After six weeks on an herbal compound and nutritional support customized to Foxy's specific condition, we saw major progress. Over the next year, Foxy healed completely, with his feet the last part to resolve. This change occurred with no antibiotic therapy whatsoever. It appears that Foxy's immune system was indeed capable of handling this bacterial infection and that by supporting his natural immune system's ability to handle the situation we allowed him to triumph over the disease process.

What caused Foxy's situation? No one knows entirely, but we can assume that something unbalanced his biological protection system and that natural therapy assisted him in rebalancing and ending the problem.

Sometimes people get upset with me because I publish stories like this one without saying exactly what we used, but I find that each case is unique and when we try to treat all dogs that look like Foxy with this same combination, it simply doesn't work. Healing requires finding the precise set of treatments that are needed for each specific pet's condition, and this varies greatly from case to case. No two cases are ever identical, even though they may look the same.

Maintaining Balance—Good and Bad

Natural healing helps the body maintain biologically desirable balances. The body is in a constant state of change. The big trick is to get these constantly fluctuating changes to center on an equilibrium that favors the body's survival. Body temperature is one example. Take your pet's temperature (or your own, for that matter) and you will find that it rises and falls within a normal range for you. Temperatures tend to be lower in the morning and then rise through the day.

Many other things fluctuate. In fact, most things in the body do this.

One of the most significant goals of natural therapies is to set this fluctuation in motion and allow the body's natural self-controlling, or autoregulatory, mechanisms to begin to take over normal function. Symptoms will arise and will improve and worsen as this happens. We frequently see this when treating allergic or other skin problems. A proper prescription often leads to itching that is worse than before. This is because the skin has begun to offload toxins and use inflammation to remove them from the area. Over time this tends to modulate and get better. The trick is to know when to do something and when to let it ride. That is not always an easy thing. For instance, in many cases it can take from one to three years for skin cases to complete this cycle and settle into a healthier state.

An important fluctuation occurs in body acid levels. The body's acidity varies greatly, and these variations (called pH) are essential to health. In humans, our tissues remain acid from 11:00 p.m. until 3:00 p.m. each day. During this acid phase, the body cleanses itself of waste by breaking down protein fibers and liquefying the gel between cells. This allows the immune system's cells to easily migrate through and ingest undesirable materials between cells. If this didn't happen, the immune cells, which are a sort of a police officer-janitor combination, would not have easy access to the tissues. From 3:00 p.m. until 11:00 p.m the body becomes alkaline and the gel between the cells actually solidifies. This is when the tissue becomes more solid as a result of orders placed earlier in response to active periods. Waste is removed in the acid phase and protein structure is laid down for support in the alkaline phase. This is a common reason why people become sleepy at 3:00 p.m.; this is the time the body wants to rest a bit for repair, a biological fact that explains why siestas, afternoon naps, are so healthy. We do not have data for these acidity variations in animals, but we can assume they are similar. Is it possible that these variations are reversed in nocturnal animals such as cats? We simply do not know at this time, but we likely see similar natural regulatory cycles in all major species. As we learn more about these cycles we may well be able to resolve other chronic conditions.

We know that good balance occurs when the body is handling itself properly and bad balance occurs when the body is not handling itself. A body that is still and unchanging is usually not a healthy one, which means we need to learn to welcome symptoms as signs and messages that instruct us about what is needed by the body to heal.

Balance really is everything, but just like a couple of kids on a teeter-totter, things rarely stay still in perfect balance. Frankly, things go up and down, as do our pet's requirements for hormones, immune cells, and nutrients.

Whether something is good or bad depends upon what the body needs at that precise moment in time. It is all relative to the needs of the body. Too much of anything is a bad thing, as is too little. Balance depends upon requirements, and these change regularly in functional disease.

Once a person recognizes this as truth it becomes very evident that taking a fixed formula multivitamin or herbal preparation is not proper nutrition because the body simply isn't getting the optimum levels of all things needed. Customizing health care by use of muscle response testing allows us to ask the body directly and measure the effect of different supplements so that we have a better chance of getting this optimal balance established. When that happens healing occurs in a much more predictable manner.

Now let's examine some common complementary and alternative veterinary medical tools we use to assist the body to recover and maintain health:

Acupuncture

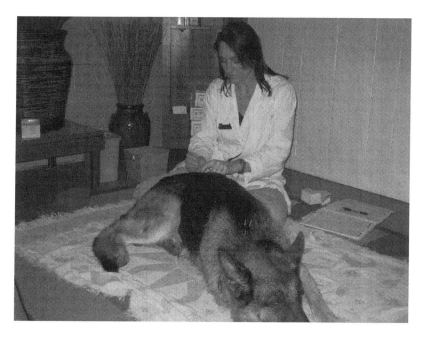

Energy runs through the body in predictable channels as it works. An acupuncturist can correct the flow of energy and assist the body in re-establishing proper levels of com-munication with various body parts by inserting needles; applying pressure, heat, or light; or injecting fluids into these channels and their control points. Acupuncture is useful for controlling pain, stimulating blood flow, draining congested fluid channels, and supporting proper immune function. It usually must be performed several times for best results. Because of the massive amounts of research going on in this field, acupuncture is now a widely respected branch of medicine with many veterinarians becoming certified in advanced techniques.

Like acupuncture, the idea of organ pairs is an impor-tant Oriental medical concept. The body is an energy system that uses paired organs to perform specific func-tions. These organ pairs are important in diagnosis and treatment because disease often appears in one organ when the other half of the pair is weak or oversupplied with energy. Correct treatment can lead to rapid improve-ment in some cases. The table below shows the organ pairs and their relationships to the seasons and body functions. Knowing this information assists your veterinarian in selecting appropriate medicines and nutritional items to support, drain, and detoxify your pet's major organ systems.

Chinese Organ Pair	Season	Regulates	Functions
Liver, Gallbladder	Spring	Stores blood Tendons/ligaments Small muscles Peripheral nerves External genitals Nails Bile/tears	Stores blood Regulates Qi Moves up and out
Heart, Small Intestine	Early summer	Arteries Complexion Tongue External ears Eye corners Blood/sweat	Propels blood
Spleen, Stomach	Late summer	Large muscles Flesh Lips, mouth Eyelids Lymph, saliva, blood	Generates and distributes nutrients Holds in and up
Lung, Large Intestine	Autumn	Nose, sinus Throat, bronchi Skin, hair Sclera of eye Mucus	Receives and distributes Qi Defenses Rhythm Boundaries
Kidney, Bladder	Winter	Ovary, teste Brain, spinal cord Bone, teeth Bone barrow Pupil, anus, urethra Head	Stores Essence Anchors Qi Balances fluids

Table 7.1. The relationship between major Chinese organ pairs and health manifestations. Notice that diseases tend to appear during the organ's time of the year, such as bronchitis during autumn and blocked urethras in cats during winter. Many other relationships between these organ pairs influence health and disease symptoms.

Herbal Medicine

Herbs, which have chemical and energetic effects, are massively useful in healing. Our modern pharmaceutical industry depends upon herbal medicine and tradition to identify useful compounds for further development into drugs. The use of various plant parts forms the foundation of many traditional healing techniques. For example, hawthorn has been used to support heart patients for centuries, and this plant is still widely used by veterinarians for heart disease. Many good studies support this use too. Plants develop compounds that help them survive, and these compounds can be used to perform many functions in health care. Herbs can be used to drain toxic fluids; fight pathogens such as bacteria, viruses, and fungi; reduce inflammation; and build organs and tissues. Although herbs are natural, they are not necessarily safe, and a wise person uses a professional who is knowledgeable about herbs for his or her proper prescription. The improper use or combination of herbs with other herbs or various drugs can lead to toxic reactions. Contamination and alteration are also common problems with herbs, so it is important to purchase herbs from manufacturers that follow ethical business models.

Homeopathy

The basic principle of homeopathy is the idea that "like cures like," and thus this area of medicine uses small amounts of agents whose toxic symptoms match the symptoms and signs that are exhibited by the patient. Individual medicines are tested by volunteers who ingest them and make detailed notes of their responses. The toxic effects observed become the symptom picture set for which a medicine has useful application. For instance, Nux vomica is a nut that contains very toxic agents that cause nausea when ingested. It also may cause anger. When Nux vomica is diluted to very low levels and administered to someone who is suffering from vomiting and anger, the disease process may simply vanish in a short time.

Homeopathy has been a popular holistic therapy for years, and thousands of people and animals have been assisted in this manner. It became controversial for several reasons, but mostly because no one could explain how it worked. As scientific study continues, we now know at least a part of the answer to this question☐it appears that these toxic substances gently stimulate natural body processes that lead patients toward healing. They act by complex mechanisms to stimulate cellular receptors and inhibit and stimulate regulatory processes, leading to activation of the patient's own immune response and recovery.

Homotoxicology, Biopuncture, and Blood Therapy

Homotoxicology is based on the hypothesis that most illness is the body's attempt to isolate, excrete, or handle homotoxins (anything that is toxic to humans). Illness is a very specific response by the body to protect itself. In homotoxicology, medicines that help the body eliminate toxins, drain toxic fluids, and build organ function are formulated and used in homeopathic dilution.

Homotoxicology has been called "modern homeopathy," but this term is not meant to denigrate traditional or classical homeopathy, as discussed above. Homotoxicology is actually a bridge between conventional medicine and holistic medicine because it uses modern diagnostic principles to direct therapy with natural homeopathic and herbal agents. These agents can be injected into acupuncture points, a very useful form of therapy known as biopuncture. Homeopathic remedies can be mixed with a patient's blood before injecting the combined material back into the patient, a treatment called "autosanguis therapy." This therapy appears to activate powerful immune reactions that can assist in recovery from a wide variety of conditions, and it can be a powerful tool for treating chronic diseases. The use of homotoxicology is growing rapidly in both Europe and the United States.

Chiropractic

Chiropractic adjustments attempt to realign the body when it has fallen into aberrant structure and function.

When body parts shift they can alter the flow of fluids and energy, leading to lowered health status. Healing can begin when affected areas are located and placed back into their optimal positions.

Craniosacral and Myofascial Release Therapies

The brain and spinal cord are bathed in a fluid called cerebrospinal fluid. This fluid moves like a tide through the body and restrictions in its flow can lead to signs of disease, according to the founder of craniosacral therapy, an osteopath named Dr. William G. Sutherland. Practitioners use a gentle touch to balance this flow within the body. It can be used in many instances but is found to be helpful in insomnia, painful issues, headaches, and other chronic diseases. Craniosacral therapy and myofascial release techniques are also thought to assist in releasing emotion and trauma that become trapped in the connective tissue.

Nutrition Response Testing℠ and Muscle Response Testing

Nutrition Response Testing℠ and Muscle Response Testing (MRT) are discussed in detail earlier in this text. Please see Chapter 4 for more information. The following summary is provided for those who have not read that chapter and those who need information about other techniques of muscle response testing beside Nutrition Response Testing℠. Biological systems have innate wisdom and intelligence. Muscle strength is affected by many subtle things. It has been observed that placing certain supplements near the body makes the muscle strength increase or decrease. When properly used, muscle response testing is NOT a diagnostic tool, but rather another way to assess and assist skilled clinicians in selecting optimal therapy for a patient. Nutrition Response Testing℠ is a technique that was organized and developed by Dr. Freddie Ulan and his partner and is the method used in our clinic. One very important aspect of Nutrition Response Testing℠ is the fact that not all patients can be tested accurately with Muscle Response Testing. By using Nutrition Response Testing^{SM} we find that many problems can be isolated and repaired so that a greater percentage of patients can be properly tested. Not all forms of muscle response testing are the same and many forms may give varied results, so use a practitioner whose skills you are confident in when using MRT or Nutrition Response Testing^{SM}. In my experience, the Nutrition Response Testing^{SM} process seems more dependable than other techniques we have examined.

Essential Oil Therapy

Essential oils contain powerful agents that can assist our animals in their quest for better health. They bring oxygen to tissues; combat fungi, bacteria, and viruses; remove environmental pollutants from cells; and perform a host of other healing functions.

That said, it is very important to follow strict guidelines when using oils on animals. First, it is critically important to use therapeutic grade oils such as those produced by Young Living Essential Oils. It is also important to know that oils can be toxic to animals and should not be applied directly to them based solely on their normal uses for people. For instance, oregano oil is toxic to cats because their livers cannot properly handle the phenolic compounds contained in the oil. Do not put oils directly in the eyes or ears or on the foot soles without veterinary instruction. If essential oils are accidentally placed into a sensitive part of the body, apply vegetable oil to remove the residue. Do not use water to remove the residue because it can drive the oils into the body. Soap and water can also be used also to cleanse skin after the area has been treated with vegetable oil and allowed to soak for a few minutes. Do not put oils on areas that are not clean and free of chemical contamination because they can move toxins directly into the blood stream. Oils should be diluted when used on dogs and cats.

Also note that animals have a much more sensitive sense of smell, so improper use of oils can actually stress them. Always give your pet a way out of oil fumes.

If your veterinarian has obtained special training, he or she should be able to assist you in the selection and proper application of oils. Those who are familiar with the use of oils in animals can use special application techniques such as raindrop therapy, which involves special application along the spine of your pet. Neuroauricular therapy uses oils to stimulate the nervous system, improve circulation, and assist in the removal of toxins.

Ozone

When normal oxygen (O_2) is exposed to high energy it becomes ozone, an unstable and reactive molecule that consists of three oxygen atoms (O_3). Ozone can be infused into the blood or tissues or inhaled to cause inflammation, increased oxygenation, and increased oxidation that can assist recovery in many situations. It should be noted that ozone is a toxic substance capable of aggravating asthma and allergies. Ozone can chemically burn delicate tissues. Its use should be monitored by a trained veterinarian.

Animal Communication

Although many scam artists claim to be able to communicate with animals, we all have some ability in this area. There are skilled individuals who can bridge the communication gap with animals, and these people can be very helpful in handling complicated medical or behavioral situations with pets. The animal communicator we use in our office has assisted us with arriving at correct diagnoses, solved emotional upsets, and helped with many other issues. When you choose to use an animal communicator, choose an individual with a good reputation and always make sure that the information you receive makes sense before you act on it.

Bach Flower Therapy

Dilute preparations of various flower essences are useful for improving patient comfort and emotional states. These remedies can be very helpful in handling behavioral issues and chronic disease states. We find them useful in behavioral issues. A common Bach Flower remedy is called Rescue remedy and is helpful for pets under stress. We commonly use this on animals that are afraid to travel to the veterinarian or when people are leaving town.

Nambudripad's Allergy Elimination Technique

Nambudripad's Allergy Elimination Technique (NAET), a technique that Dr. Devi S. Nambudripad began teaching less than thirty years ago, employs a variation of muscle response testing to identify allergens. These can be environmental substances, foods, chemicals, forms of energy, concepts, or parts of the patient's own body (i.e., autoimmune or immune-mediated responses) that elicit inappropriate hypersensitivities or allergies. Once identified, these hypersensitivities or allergies can usually be eliminated or desensitized within twenty-five hours. They may return after a period of time.

To eliminate the allergy, the NAET practitioner has the patient hold the allergen or its energetic equivalent in hand (or attaches it to a pet's collar, etc.) while correcting the spinal subluxations caused by the allergen as part of its clinical expression. The NAET practitioner uses a simple acupressure technique, which involves digital pressure or the application of an "activator"—a device commonly used by chiropractors—to correct the spinal subluxation. The patient then remains in contact with the allergen for twenty minutes, and then avoids it for the subsequent twenty-five hours. The patient is checked again for allergies after the twenty-five-hour hour clearing period, and it is expected that the patient will then be able to confront the allergen without adverse reaction.

Locating Practitioners

To locate practitioners who use any of the above modalities, visit the Web site of the American Holistic Veterinary Medical Association at www.ahvma.org. Click on the "find a holistic vet" link and search by zip codes or names for doctors in your area.

> *Integrative medicine takes advantage of all available knowledge in selecting tools appropriate for healing. Having more tools gives an improved chance for success.*

Chapter 8. Rejuvenation Therapy: Stem Cells

Stem cells are primitive cells that live in your pet's body. They are essential for maintenance and repair. Many of us are familiar with the controversy surrounding embryonic stem cell research. While this seems to be a popular topic for political debate, it really has very little real-world application. Embryonic stem cells originate in an embryo with a unique DNA structure from any other person. As such, when attempts are made to use these cells in healthy people, they lead to wild outcomes such as teratomas (a form of tumor consisting of teeth, hair, and other tissues growing like some monster from a zombie/mad scientist movie).

The stem cells we are talking about here are called "autologous" stem cells, the stem cells that are made by your pet's own body and whose purpose is to repair and maintain that very same body. These cells are specific for only your pet and no other. While the use of stem cells that come from embryos is controversial, ineffective, and dangerous in many instances, the use of stem cells that originate from your pet's own normal tissues is a highly effective means of assisting recovery from chronic diseases such as arthritis, tendinitis, liver disease, scars, and fractures.

As the science of stem cells develops, other applications may be found, such as neurologic disease (trauma and stroke), heart disease, diabetes, and kidney disease. In the meantime, our office is credentialed to deliver this exciting high-tech option for healing and we are happy to provide you with information about the use of your pet's own stem cells. Vet-Stem, the company doing most stem cell work in the United States can help interested people find a veterinarian in their area.

> "Almost immediately after her stem cell transplant, Luci was back to her bouncy, happy self."
>
> Shirley Zindler
> Santa Rosa, CA

Stem cells live in many tissues, but there is a massive population of these cells in fatty tissue. By harvesting a small amount of fat, we can purify and collect these stem cells and then inject them directly back into affected tissues. Once injected, your pet's own stem cells release biologically active chemicals, which directly reduce inflammation and pain while assisting in natural repair. They also prevent early cell death, something that is critical in certain injuries such as heart attacks and neurological traumas (disc disease and stroke). Stem cells also release special chemicals that attract other healing cells to the area, and they appear to regulate localized healing. Some stem cells differentiate and grow into many different types of cells (connective tissue, blood vessels, immune cells, and others) that are needed for tissue repair.

Stem cells can be activated by many means. For years our office has worked with natural methods of healing that appear to directly activate these healing cells. Acupuncture, homotoxicology, autogenous blood therapy, and other natural methods of healing may help with this activation. For instance, recent research has shown that certain nutrients may directly cause increased release of these important cells. When these gentle therapies don't handle the situation, the use of stem cell transplants may be useful.

The technique is fairly simple to understand. After an evaluation of your pet that includes a history, physical exam, and appropriate laboratory testing, an appointment is made for stem cell harvesting. Timing is important. If your pet is particularly inactive or ill, certain steps may need to be taken to get it into condition for the procedure. Stem cell numbers are increased by exercise and decreased by disease and steroid therapy, so a program is created to make this procedure as effective as possible. Generally no steroids should be given before or within forty-five days of the procedure. NSAID pain medications are acceptable, but herbal agents and acupuncture are better in many cases.

On day one of the Vet Stem® transplant procedure, a small amount of fat is harvested by a surgeon and sent to the stem cell laboratory for processing. The next day it is express mailed to our hospital, and on the third or fourth day it is injected into your pet. Sedation may or may not be needed for the injection process.

Below are some frequently asked questions about Vet-Stem® stem cell therapy from the Vet Stem web site (www.vet-stem.com). If your interest in this topic is low, I suggest you skip over this slightly more technical part, and come back to it if you ever have questions regarding the procedure.

Do Regenerative Stem Cells Cure Degenerative Joint Disease (Osteoarthritis)?

Because of the ongoing nature of arthritic changes, regenerative stem cells may not permanently stop the degenerative processes. However, intra-articular regenerative stem cell administration may provide long-term anti-inflammatory effects, decrease pain, stimulate regeneration of cartilage tissue that slows the degenerative processes, and initiate healing in chronic and acute injuries. Some cases require periodic treatment with stored (banked) doses of cells. Successful uses have been documented for most joints, and especially for difficult arthritis cases such as elbow, hip, shoulder, and knee osteoarthritis.

Can I Store My Animal's Cells?

Absolutely. The Vet-Stem® bank service is a specially designed tissue preservation process that prepares your animal's regenerative stem cells for long-term storage in liquid nitrogen containers.

Why Is This Form of Stem Cell Therapy So Desirable?

Vet-Stem Regenerative Cells (VSRCs):

- Contain high yield of stem cells
- Contain many other regenerative cells that produce active compounds that assist healing and repair
- Are able to differentiate into many different types of cells needed for repair
- Produce building blocks that support cells structurally
- Are taken from your animal's own fat so there is no chance of cancer development or rejection, as with stem cells that come from embryos. Furthermore, no embryos are harmed in this process.
- Cells available for treatment within forty-eight hours

How Does Regenerative Cell Therapy Improve the Time and Quality of Injury Healing?

Osteoarthritis: Clinical improvement is typically seen very quickly, often within a few days to a few weeks after initiation of regenerative cell therapy. Owners report that patients continue to improve as healing progresses.

- Tendons and ligaments: Because soft tissue injuries vary widely according to the amount of damage and the age of the injury and the animal, healing time is variable regardless of the modality of therapy. The regenerative cell therapy of Vet-Stem® significantly improves the quality of healing.
- Fractures: Healing of skeletal fractures is greatly enhanced with regenerative cell therapy; decreased fracture size and clinical improvement occur in approximately half the time of normal fracture healing rates. A rehabilitation program is an important component to facilitate adequate healing.

How Many Doses Are Required For Success?

Veterinarians have found tendon and ligament injuries usually respond to a single dose. Due to the chronic nature of degenerative joint disease (osteoarthritis), additional doses may be required at varying intervals depending on severity, which joint is affected, and the use of the animal.

What Other Medications or Treatments Can Be Given at the Same Time?

Nonsteroidal anti-inflammatories (NSAIDS): Concurrent use is acceptable, but we attempt to reduce their use in our office due to a wide number of potential negative side effects.

- Hyaluronic acid (HA): Has been shown to enhance the use of stem and regenerative cells
- Glucosamine and/or chondroitin sulfate: Concurrent use is acceptable
- Acupuncture: Concurrent use is acceptable
- Magnetic therapy: Concurrent use is acceptable
- Antibiotics: Concurrent use of systemic antibiotics as prescribed by the attending veterinarian is acceptable

Is the Tissue Source of Stem Cells Important?

This field is constantly developing. It is now well established in the scientific community that there is a high concentration of mesenchymal stem cells in fat–one hundred to five hundred times more than in a bone marrow aspirate. It is advantageous to use fat-derived regenerative stem cells because culturing to increase cell numbers is not necessary. As a result, cells can be returned in forty-eight hours rather than several weeks, a critical time for healing of acute injuries before scar tissue has formed.

Early in stem cell research, the only available source of stem cells was believed to be embryos (fertilized eggs). This source is still quite controversial, because an embryo is destroyed to obtain the stem cells. Later, researchers believed that bone marrow was the only other source of stem cells. Since the late 1990s, however, new sources of stem cells have been discovered that are capable of being transformed into most of the major types of cells found in tissues throughout the body.

Future Uses of Regenerative Stem Cells

The following uses are being evaluated in small animals:
- Heart disease
- Liver disease
- Kidney disease
- Neurologic disease
- Immune-mediated disease

✬ ✬ ✬

Chapter 9. Vaccinations

Killer diseases exist in this world. Parvovirus is a terrible disease of young dogs that attacks their intestinal tracts and wipes out their immune systems. The death rate in unvaccinated puppies is high. Canine distemper virus attacks a puppy's entire body, causing diarrhea, pneumonia, and fatal neurological complications. It can leave dogs blind or permanently damaged neurologically. Cats are similarly stricken by many serious viruses. Herpes virus causes permanent damage to many cats. Feline leukemia and immunodeficiency virus wipe out cats' immune systems, leaving them prone to anemia, cancer, and death.

Anyone who has watched a puppy or kitten die of such diseases knows that vaccination is one of the most significant developments of the last century. Countries that don't use these vaccinations suffer from massive health issues. In China, where less than 3 percent of the dogs are vaccinated for rabies, the government recently killed fifty thousand dogs in an attempt to control a serious rabies epidemic. Here in Los Angeles, California, people forget that just a few decades ago we had rabid dogs running in our streets. While we still have rabies in our wildlife populations, the vaccine program stopped the earlier epidemics and drastically reduced human exposure.

Vaccinations unquestionably reduce the rates of death and disfigurement from these nasty diseases. In our practice we never see cases of parvovirus or feline distemper in vaccinated pets. Vaccines make our streets safer for other pets and our children. Immunizations are important modern tools for protecting the health and well-being of our pets; however, they are not without complications. Pet guardians need accurate information to make decisions about their pets' health care, and vaccinations are no exception.

Animal owners and veterinarians alike are paying much more attention to the proper use of vaccinations. Our office began advocating reform of vaccination protocols many years ago and now large veterinary groups such as the American Animal Hospital Association recommend reducing the number and frequency of commonly used vaccines for both dogs and cats. We applaud this effort and encourage the profession to expand its research in this important part of veterinary care.

Like all things in a medical practice, vaccine protocols must be individually crafted for each pet. Each has a unique genetic makeup and particular risk factors for various diseases, and these must be considered in formulating vaccine programs. Vaccination is, after all, a medical procedure and deserves the same level of consideration and concern as any other serious health care decision.

Vaccines stimulate the immune system to produce antibody and cellular responses to germs that can cause significant diseases. To create a vaccine, the virus or bacteria is either killed or modified in one way or another so that the majority of patients can safely take it. A small immune response occurs on the first vaccine and then a larger, more long-lasting response occurs after the second vaccine. This response varies by vaccine type, disease type, and the strength of the animal receiving the vaccination.

There are three types of vaccines:

1. Killed vaccines, wherein the disease-causing germ has been killed and rendered unable to cause infection. These vaccines use chemicals called adjuvants to stimulate stronger immune reactions, and these chemical adjuvants may cause increased likelihood of vaccine reactions and even cancer. They usually bring about weaker and shorter immunity than other vaccines.
2. Modified live vaccines, in which the virus has been treated in such a way that it cannot infect and cause life-threatening disease.
3. Recombinant vaccines, which use the genetic material of other viruses, such as the bird poxvirus, to transmit information to the immune system.

The clinician and animal guardian should consider the proper timing for vaccine administration so optimum immunity results and adverse reactions are minimized. Puppies' and kittens' mothers pass protective proteins, called antibodies, to them soon after birth. Therefore, an early vaccine may not succeed in reaching the pet's immune system, resulting in a vaccine failure. Repeating vaccines at intervals is necessary to bring about dependable protection against disease.

Concurrent environmental or medical factors may affect patient response to vaccination. Many vaccines carry the statement in their packaging "for use in healthy animals only." This is wise advice because vaccination during periods of illness may negatively affect patient response. It is not known if administration of vaccines during illness increases the risk of other adverse events, such as immune imbalance, but common sense suggests that we ensure a pet is healthy before challenging its immune system. Concurrent administration of drugs, particularly those that affect the immune system, such as steroids and nonsteroidal anti-inflammatories, may alter the response to vaccination and should be avoided if possible. A study in mice showed decreased response to vaccinations given when NSAIDs were present.

Vaccines for canine distemper and parvovirus probably last for a very long time. For this reason many veterinarians draw blood and test for antibody levels. This testing is called "titering," and the results demonstrate the presence of protective antibodies, indicating a vaccine response. This works well for some diseases but not for others. Titering is very useful for dogs but less so for cats. Diseases vary by location and your veterinarian can help you decide which diseases are real risks for your pet and which don't require protection. This is an important reason to have a personal relationship with a veterinarian that you trust to give you accurate and truthful information.

No vaccine protects 100 percent of those animals that receive it and no vaccine is free of side effects. The most common reactions are mild fevers and inflammation at the site of injection, but other more severe reactions can occur. We advise that owners stay with their pets for at least one hour after vaccination. Life-threatening reactions are rare and usually occur within about thirty minutes. If a strange reaction occurs following vaccination you should report this to the doctor as soon as possible. If your pet shows more serious symptoms you should go to the doctor immediately for emergency care.

One of our greatest concerns about vaccinations involves the presence of other substances in the vaccine. Pharmaceutical companies are not required to reveal the contents of vaccines and so other toxic agents may be present. Mercury is a well known vaccine ingredient that is used to prevent bacterial contamination. It has been shown to increase the chances of self target immune responses in people and we assume the same is true of pets. It is best to avoid excessive administration of these compounds. One form of mercury is known as thimerosal, and our practice uses thimerosal-free rabies vaccines.

Because patients use their immune systems to respond to vaccines, it is best to take steps to strengthen your pet's immune system during their puppy or kitten vaccines. Integrative doctors often recommend nutritional support of the immune system to enhance the response and reduce the severity of reactions to vaccines. In our office we encourage these support substances and feel that we see fewer problems since we began using glandular and whole food support of our pediatric patients.

The important vaccines that are recommended for most dogs include canine distemper virus, canine parvovirus, hepatitis virus (also called adenovirus), and rabies virus. Vaccines for Lyme and Bordatella are optional and based upon patient risk factors. Leptospirosis is a bacterial disease that is spread from wildlife. It can cause significant liver and kidney disease. This vaccine is recommended in high-risk areas but it carries its own high risk of more serious reactions and we do not use it routinely in our practice.

All cats should receive kitten vaccines for distemper, herpes, chlamydia, and calicivirus. Booster shots are recommended every three years. The rabies vaccine is recommended once in most cats' lives, but it can cause fibrosarcoma and must be used with proper understanding. In many states a cat that bites someone and is unprotected for rabies must be euthanized and tested for rabies. It can be quarantined if it has been vaccinated for rabies, which is much more desirable. Vaccination for feline leukemia virus is recommended only for cats that have outdoor contact because this vaccine can also cause fibrosarcoma (a fatal form of cancer). The vaccine for the feline AIDs virus, called

FIV, is not recommended for indoor cats and will cause any cat that has been vaccinated to test as if it has the more serious form of the disease. We do not recommend this vaccine at this time. Cats older than ten or eleven years of age need special consideration; owners may elect to reduce their vaccination after discussion with their doctors.

Vaccines are important in disease prevention, but they can cause health problems. Giving unnecessary or redundant vaccines does not protect a pet further, but may expose it to potentially dangerous factors. Discuss vaccines with your doctor and only use those that directly apply to your pet's health history and environmental risks.

✿ ✿ ✿

Chapter 10. Working with Health Care Professionals

The Doctor-Client Relationship

This admonishment "Seek Truth and healing follows" extends to professional relationships. Do everything in your power to maintain truthful, friendly relationships with your veterinary professional. Telling the truth, the whole truth, and nothing but the truth is the best policy on both sides of the examination table. Be honest about your resources and your desires and goals for health care because this really assists your doctor in treatment planning and diagnosis. If you are afraid to tell the doctor something, then you need to evaluate your relationship with the clinic. You should feel safe telling your doctor anything that seems important to your pet's care.

Veterinarians have studied many thousands of hours to become licensed professionals. We do that because we want to do the best job possible for you and your pet. We are armed with many modern technologies and knowledge about how to best use them.

You are deeply devoted to your pet's health care and well-being. Depending upon many other factors, you may have access to a wealth of health care information and resources as well.

Together with your pet we form a health care team. Each member of this team has a responsibility and a job, and if we all understand this we become more effective in delivering the best health care possible.

This functions best with totally open communication and mutual respect. The word "respect" literally means "to look again," and this suggests that if we find ourselves not liking or not respecting our fellows, then we need to take a moment, stop, and look again so that everything is properly oriented. For example, your doctor wants to deliver the best health care possible to your pet. To do this he observes and correlates his findings with the massive volume of education available. He integrates this information with his own experience and arrives at a recommended treatment plan. Sometimes a client becomes upset when the doctor explains his treatment plan. This is the precise point at which respect come into play. If these two people respect each other, instead of trading harsh words and going their separate ways, they can continue to communicate and hopefully come closer to solving the pet's health dilemma.

The doctor-client relationship is a two-way street. The veterinarian must clearly understand the client's goals. The client must understand the veterinarian's goals and purposes. The two must appreciate and respect the other's abilities and then coordinate efforts to solve many difficult situations. If either party falls short, then the pet may pay the price and this is not what anyone wants.

Veterinarians are experts in an area of care, but we are still humans. We come in all sizes and beliefs and have differing abilities, knowledge bases, and experience. The best doctors know that they don't know it all and work constantly to improve their knowledge. And since no one person can know it all, the best veterinarians surround themselves with other really competent experts. As humans, though, we all have good days and bad days. It can be difficult to see one emergency after another, or to work through a day when four of your favorite elder pets pass away. Likewise, it can be nearly impossible to balance time considerations and medical quality, but most veterinarians I know work very hard to do these things.

Have compassion for your doctor and he or she will return it.

Communication Is Key

Not all doctors agree on how to handle similar cases. There is art to medicine, and changing doctors too frequently can really confuse a medical case. If you are seeing more than one veterinarian or health care practitioner, be sure to tell your veterinarian and have him or her share information about treatment plans, medication, and test results. Not only can this get you better results for your dollar, it can actually prevent costly duplication of effort and potentially dangerous drug interactions. Never withhold from your conventional doctor what complementary treatments your pet is receiving. Likewise, be sure your integrative or holistic doctors know all of the drugs and other treatments you are using. Drugs and herbs can interact badly and this is less likely to occur when all parties know what is happening with your pet's care.

Your veterinarian should listen to you and attempt to answer your questions. If you hear a word or concept that you don't understand, please stop the conversation and clear it up, because things will not get clearer as the conversation goes forward. Misunderstood words can lead to confusion and disagreement, and they must be kept to a minimum. It takes work by both the client and professional to achieve really effective communication, but it is well worth the effort!

Remember that while we are a health care team, ultimately you, the owner, are the captain, and you must be involved in the decision-making process. If you have questions, comments, or suggestions, share them with your doctor and the professional team. If things make sense, then we are usually working on the Truth line, but if you are confused or feeling overwhelmed, tell your doctor and take a moment to sort things out. Truth works and it's worth finding and working with in all realms of Life.

> *Good manners and truthful conduct work hand in hand in any relationship.*

✲ ✲ ✲

Chapter 11. Using Drugs Wisely

Understanding Drug Use

Scientific development of effective drugs in the twentieth century truly is one of the most important milestones in modern medicine. Drugs are not evil. They improve the quality and quantity of our lives and those of our friends and families, not to mention our pets. However, in the process of discovering better and better drugs, our society and medical professionals seemed to lose their desire to discover fundamental causes for diseases. The emphasis shifted from cure and prevention to symptom suppression. Because all drugs have adverse effects, we must always question the use of drugs and look for safer alternatives that may actually assist in reversing disease. This is a major reason for the growing popularity of the integrative veterinary medicine movement.

Drugs are an important part of therapy plans in our practice, but nutritional, glandular supplements and herbal, and homeopathic medicines lead the way as useful tools in our healing toolbox. Using nutritional, antihomotoxic, herbal, and homeopathic agents allows us to intervene effectively much earlier in the development of disease. It is likely that some diseases never manifest or that they occur later when these agents are used properly. Preventative medicine takes on an entirely different face when these tools are applied. Knowing some basic facts about drugs and their use will help you to better understand their potential effects on your pet, and may prove to be helpful in discussions with your veterinarian.

How Drugs Work

All drugs interfere with natural processes by blocking biological control factors and influencing them in one way or another. Some basic mechanisms of actions by pharmaceutical agents are:

- Stimulate receptors
- Block receptors
- Block enzymes
- Stimulate cell functions
- Suppress cell functions
- Replace missing essential biological substances such as hormones or nutrients

These activities cause dose-dependent responses by bodies. Small doses stimulate functions, and slightly higher doses stimulate even more strongly, but higher doses eventually suppress these natural processes. Extremely high doses lead to more severe suppression and even death. As a result of these alterations in natural mechanisms, all drugs can lead to adverse effects (also called side effects). Natural compounds can also do this.

Drugs work outside the body's natural control system, so they can bypass the normal control mechanisms of the body. It is by knocking the complex system of controls out of balance that drugs cause many side effects. Because scientists do not fully understand the complexity of this system, and because similar molecules can be involved in many different tissues, it is possible for a drug to cause one good effect but damage the body in other unknown ways that don't always appear until later in the pet's life.

NSAIDs are good examples of this. These drugs are commonly used in conventional practice to treat pain and arthritis. Many doctors use these drugs following surgery because they reduce pain, but many don't know that they also may decrease wound healing or cause delayed fracture repair. They can also damage the liver, kidneys, or intestines. This damage often occurs without the patient knowing it; suddenly he becomes ill with other symptoms such as vomiting, diarrhea, or bleeding after taking these medications. NSAIDs should be used only when needed and only in the lowest dosage and for the shortest time possible.

Truthfully, many of these adverse effects are the body's attempt to remove the toxic drug from its system—this is why so many drugs cause vomiting and diarrhea. Headaches, skin rashes, unexplained pain, and other symptoms are also sometimes signs that the body is trying to remove the drug. Pain and discomfort are signs of disease, and damage to the body done by drugs can cause these symptoms to appear as a warning to the patient. This should alert the patient that drugs are only a temporary solution in many cases, and that searching for curative agents is often the best path to follow.

Dr. Sara Pettitt, a licensed acupuncturist and very able Nutrition Response Testing℠ practitioner here in Los Angeles, pointed out to me that in her human health care practice she often sees drugs as "enablers." An enabler is a psychological term for someone or something that allows or makes it easier for a person to continue in a harmful or destructive fashion. It is often used when discussing addicts. Prescription drugs can be enablers; they allow a person to continue to do a harmful action without the apparent physical consequence. As an example, a person acts badly, feels guilty, and then takes antidepressants without changing his behavior. The drug causes him to feel less emotion, but also makes him toxic. This toxicity makes him feel worse and eventually his illness worsens. While such drug use keeps people alive, it can reduce their demand to find the correct cause of their illness and thus resolve it.

I experienced this personally while dealing with high blood pressure. Because I worked long hours and didn't like to exercise, I sought Dr. Pettitt's advice in hopes of finding some nutritional or homeopathic agents that would lower my blood pressure. In human medicine it is known that only 19 percent of the people who opt for blood pressure medications as their sole high blood pressure treatment get good control, whereas more than 80 percent can obtain control of their blood pressure by diet, weight loss, and exercise. I wanted another solution, but truthfully, until I began to exercise every day for thirty minutes and eat a proper diet, my blood pressure would not drop. Dr. Pettitt helped me clean up my body's basic health enough that exercise became pleasant. That took a long time for me because I was suffering from several toxic syndromes. Nutrition and diet handled each one as it came up. Finally, after getting healthy enough to begin exercising, my blood pressure dropped quickly. If I had just used drugs alone I doubt that my blood pressure would be this well controlled. Furthermore, the drugs would have enabled me to live in an unhealthy way instead of just changing my ways to create health.

Sometimes Drugs Are Necessary

Don't take this to mean that all drugs are bad, or that all illness is a punishment for bad behavior, because that simply is not true. It is true that drugs can suppress symptoms of more serious issues and prevent a person from discovering the truth needed to improve her life.

When should drugs be used? Drugs cause rapid responses and these are often needed when dealing with life-threatening conditions. If a patient is having a stroke from blood clotting, there is not time to get her living a better life-style, exercising more, and controlling her blood pressure. An emergency doctor must handle the immediate situation and the danger therein with drugs, but once the danger is handled, the patient should be more completely evaluated so that a more effective long-term program addressing the cause of the situation can be implemented.

Drugs can also prolong life when the truth of an illness remains undiscovered. Cardiac drugs are a good example. A patient who doesn't control his blood pressure has a greater chance of death from stroke or heart failure, but drugs allow him to live on in the search for better health. Hopefully, he will learn and heed his doctor's advice about taking positive steps to create health too, but if your cat's blood pressure is over 250 mm of mercury (normal should be under 160 mm of mercury), then your doctor had better get it down quickly before blood vessels rupture and lead to brain, kidney, or eye damage. Following this initial emergency treatment, we can begin to seek out why the blood pressure is high and take steps to address that as well. And it is likely that a cat with high blood pressure will need some medication as part of its treatment program because most cats with hypertension have kidney disease as the underlying reason for their high blood pressure. Patients with advanced, nonreversible disease may need these medications to stay alive. Drugs may be part of a needed program to improve health and preserve life. Over time, as understanding improves, other effective tools may replace them. In many cases the need for drugs drops as healing occurs, but not all patients can stop using pharmaceuticals.

The table below lists some commonly used drugs and their reasons for use as well as common side effects. You can find more information on the Internet and in texts such as the Physicians' Desk Reference. You can also request information on drug side effects from your veterinarian.

Prescription drugs save millions of patients each year, but they are potent substances that often work against your pet's natural care and control systems. It is therefore important to be well educated about the drugs you are giving to your pet. Monitoring blood levels may be important for effective and safe drug therapy, and your veterinarian will often advise taking this critical safety step. With appropriate integrative health programming it may be possible to reduce the levels of drugs needed as well as their side effects. Sometimes we can even eliminate a drug entirely, but this usually is done gradually so as not to shock your pet's system too greatly.

> *Knowing the technicalities about your pet's condition can help you make decisions about how to best treat its current health challenges. Using drugs properly is an important aspect of your pet's health care.*

Generic Name	Trade Name	Indications	Common Adverse Effects*
Amoxicillin	Amoxidrops	Bacterial infections	V, D; caution in pets allergic to penicillin
Amoxicillin clavulanate	Clavamox	Bacterial infections	V, D; caution in pets allergic to penicillin
Ampicillin	Omnipen	Bacterial infections	V, D; caution in pets allergic to penicillin
Doxycycline	Vibramycin	Rickettsial, protozoal, bacterial infections	V, D, esophageal ulceration
Enrofloxacin	Baytril	Bacterial infections	V, D, seizures, joint damage in young pets, liver toxicity if overdosed
Penicillin G	Generic	Infections	Penicillin allergy
Enalapril	Enacard, Vasotec	High blood pressure, heart failure, kidney tubular disease	Fainting, low blood pressure, kidney aggravation, NSAID interactions
Benazapril	Lotensin	High blood pressure, heart failure, kidney tubular disease	Fainting, low blood pressure, kidney aggravation, NSAID interactions
Prednisalone	Delta-cortef	Anti-inflammatory, allergic disease, autoimmune diseases, appetite stimulation, cancer therapy	V, D, GI bleeding, immune suppression, hormonal suppression, diabetes, hepatitis; alters blood results
Deracoxib	Deramaxx	Anti-inflammatory, arthritis, painful conditions	V, D, skin rashes and itching, GI hemorrhage, kidney and liver disease
Carprofen	Rimadyl	Anti-inflammatory, arthritis, painful conditions,	V, D, skin rashes and itching, GI hemorrhage, liver and kidney damage
L-Thyroxine	Soloxine	Thyroid insufficiency	Side effects rare and usually from overdosage; monitor blood levels regularly
Praziquantel	Droncit	Tapeworms	Vomiting at high doses; safe in pregnancy
Phenobarbital	Luminal	Seizure control	Liver disease, weight gain, appetite stimulant
Fluoxetine	Prozac Reconcile	Depression, separation anxiety	Lethargy, depression, anxiety, aggression, vomiting
Furosemide	Lasix	Diuretic, heart failure	Potassium loss, weakness
Cyclophos-phamide	Cytoxan	Lymphoid cancer	Bladder hemorrhage, immune suppression

Table 11.1. Commonly used drugs. Indications and common adverse effects. *According to manufacturer's drug label or Physicians' Desk Reference. (Abbreviations: D = diarrhea, V = vomiting)

Chapter 12. Cancer: Our Greatest Fear as Pet Owners

How Cancer Develops

Mention cancer and people's faces pale.

Their heart rates change.

The room gets quiet.

Cancer is not a fun subject and surveys show this is the number one concern of pet owners. It is an important cause of death for pets. In cats, nearly 50 percent of elderly patients die from this disease. Our ability to treat cancer and extend the lives of patients with malignant diseases has improved, but cancer rates have also risen in recent years and people are rightly concerned.

This chapter is not a comprehensive guide to treating cancer patients. It is directed at knowing how to decrease your healthy pet's chances of ever getting cancer. If your pet has cancer now, I strongly recommend that you read this material and then seek competent professional assistance as soon as possible. Some useful books are listed in the references section at the end of this book. You should read them and become an active participant in your pet's treatment plan. Integrative therapies combine modern conventional veterinary medicine with holistic approaches and can do much to assist pets with cancer.

Cancer is simply the body's misdirected effort to survive longer when conditions that favor death have developed. Injury from radiation, chemicals, viruses, toxins, chronic exposure to negative emotions, and even primary genetic errors lead to the development of abnormal cells. These cells begin to use more primitive genetic solutions to survive in the more challenging conditions present in the diseased body. In responding to these conditions (such as reduced oxygen, increased waste products, and increased acidity), the cells mutate and activate cellular systems that prevent them from dying normally. These mutations actually allow the cancer cells to survive in locations that challenge normal tissues.

> In properly functioning immune systems, these abnormal cells are rapidly handled by either repairing them or killing them. If the immune system fails, then the problem we call "cancer" begins.

Normally cells die at prescribed times and are replaced, but cancer cells activate an "immortality" gene that stops them from dying. Once this happens, a colony of cancer cells begins to grow and cancer (a tumor or leukemia) develops if the immune system fails to handle the situation. These cells carry on their surface abnormal proteins that actually announce to the body that a cancer is growing. In properly functioning immune systems, these cells are rapidly handled by either repairing them or killing them. If the immune system fails, then the problem we call "cancer" begins. It has been estimated that most of us create about ten thousand new tumors each day. We do not get cancer, though, because our healthy immune systems simply handle them as part of their daily jobs.

Modern medicine fixates on fighting the tumors and killing cancer cells, but there are steps that are taken long before the actual tumor grows, which can lead a person to cancer prevention. Knowing these simple facts can lead to decreased rates of cancer, and it is my hope that we can take steps before cancer develops in more and more pets until eventually we see the rates of cancer drop. Dr. Martin Goldstein, author of *The Nature of Animal Healing*, says, "Cancer is the ultimate reason to get well," and by this he means that proper treatment of cancer must involve those things that truly strengthen the patient's immune system because chemotherapy alone doesn't cure most cancers; in fact, it makes the body more toxic and weak. The patient, not the drug, is the source of true healing. The drugs and surgery simply buy us time to get the patient's system working better. So cancer is truly the ultimate wake-up call regarding changing one's life.

Why not strengthen the immune system and prevent this disease earlier, instead of waiting until it is already too late for many patients? Dr. Ihor Basko is a noted holistic veterinarian and elder of the American Holistic Veterinary Medical Association who lives and practices veterinary medicine in Hawaii and makes this point frequently. Prevention is more rewarding and much more cost effective. It is simply taking steps to make life easier for both you and your pet. Prevention is proactive living wherein we create conditions favorable for Life and survival and diminish those that are harmful to our survival and the survival of our beloved animal friends.

As we have said so many times in this book, "Seek truth and healing follows." It also follows that if we share truth then we decrease illness. That is the big goal in approaching conditions such as cancer. Increasing the availability of Truth leads to higher awareness. So often the ultimate cause of our problems is decreased awareness. If we increase awareness, then living systems can act more logically and we improve Life. Making our pets and ourselves healthier increases awareness. Becoming aware leads to access to life-changing information and energies. We can take steps to gradually spiral that awareness upward and spread what we find on the journey. If we do that then we all win as we improve our lives. Life as a fundamental action takes truth and uses it to improve living systems. Let's do that for cancer.

Reducing the Risk

Cancer is a devastating disease, but there are many things we can do to reduce the risk of this disease for our pets and ourselves. We must empower ourselves with correct knowledge and abandon fear which paralyzes us and makes us susceptible to error. Studies actually show that fear makes us less intelligent, while education can increase our intelligence quotient. Genetics, diet, and exercise are the most productive areas for cancer protection. Helping our pets to live healthier lives does not guarantee that they will never have cancer, but it gives us a road map to a healthier and happier place. And in the sad case when cancer does occur, pets have better survival chances when their owners are well informed and use veterinary services wisely.

Let's look at some simple choices we can make to improve the health of our pets and greatly reduce their cancer risks in the process:

❑ **Genetics:** Select a pet with a good understanding of its particular breed's cancer risk. If possible, ask the breeder about the causes of death in animals in your pet's family tree. Certain breeds have much higher cancer risks than others. Golden retrievers and Boxers are incredibly fun and loving dogs, but they have well-known high risks of cancer. Large breed dogs have higher risks for bone and splenic cancer. Pugs have higher risks for skin cancer. Purebred and long-haired cats also have higher cancer risks. White cats that live outdoors are at greater risk; so if you are selecting a pet that will live outdoors, please consider these factors. Do your research before obtaining your pet. Mixed breed dogs and cats have lower cancer risks; so rescuing a mixed breed dog may provide you with a healthier pet while reducing suffering in the world.

❑ **Exercise:** Regular exercise is linked to lower risk of several cancers in humans. It improves blood flow, opens stagnant tissues, flushes out wastes, and stimulates immune functions. Exercise also releases powerful brain chemicals that may affect your pet's immune systems in all sorts of unknown, but beneficial ways. Get outside and walk and meet other people and pets for maximum benefit. Healthy social interaction leads to improved immune system function. It makes for stronger neighborhoods too.

❑ **Diet:** The three most important things you need to know about cancer prevention and health creation are:

A. Nutrition
B. Nutrition
C. Nutrition

Proper nutrition gives the body building blocks for proper growth of normal tissues. It also provides for proper repair and excretion of wastes. Good nutrition actually helps repair damaged genetic material. Nutrition means eating real food properly, and not simply taking a ton of chemical vitamins. Vitamin pills by themselves are not nutrition. All the magical herbs and vitamin pills in the world will not correct an incomplete, bad, or destructive diet. Rather, eating a proper diet is incredibly important. Feed a great diet that is relatively free of chemical preservatives and has a variety of good, fresh ingredients. Your integrative veterinarian and pet store owner can help you select a diet—or diets—that fit your pet. Use fresh, raw, wholesome foods to supplement your pet's diet. It is fine to feed well-constructed commercial diets but realize that cooking and processing causes these foods to lose vitality and requires more work by your pet's digestive system. Your pet's immune system receives maximum nutritional support from a wide variety of different foods. In addition, feed appropriate diets for your pet's activity level.

Avoid "junk" foods such as processed meat treats, pet "jerky," artificially colored and preserved biscuits, etc. These do nothing to assist your pet's health and actually can lead to damage from poor quality or adulterated contents. Simply feed a wide variety of healthy foods and avoid junk. Think of the money you'll save.

❑ **Reduce Toxins:** Toxic or excess chemicals damage your pet's biological terrain, the microscopic environment that surrounds every cell. A healthy pet is hard to infect with bacteria, viruses, and molds, but a pet that has been fed a poor diet or has chemical toxicities finds it harder to resist infections. It also is harder to repair the damage that results from such infections, so keeping the terrain in your pet's body healthy is health care in the highest form. German doctors have long taught that most disease begins in the intracellular matrix, so caring for your pet's biological terrain before it gets diseased is the best way to operate. To date I have never seen a cancer patient that is not suffering from chemical toxicity. Do what you can to clean up the environment and you are helping create health on a broad basis.

❏ **Keep It Fresh**: Fresh air, fresh water, fresh food. If you don't put toxins into the body, then you have less work to get rid of all that trash. Avoid feeding rancid foods. Pets cannot digest rotten or rancid food properly. When normal oxygen contacts fats, they oxidize. Oxidized fats are carcinogenic and can cause inflammation due to their toxicity to the body. Flax seeds contain massive amounts of beneficial fatty acids, but when they are ground, they become rancid very quickly. If you use flax seed in your pet's diet, purchase a spice grinder or coffee grinder and grind fresh flax seed immediately before serving it to your pet. Prior to grinding, store the seeds in a sealed plastic bag in the freezer to protect their nutrients. Avoid pet treats or supplements that contain ground flax. Flax oil is very healthy; to ensure quality buy cold-pressed oil in light-resistant bottles, add 400 IU of vitamin E to the bottle for preservation, and keep it tightly sealed and refrigerated. Although fish oil is very helpful for supplementation, the quality varies widely. Be aware of heavy metal contamination of fish oil and select brands that have good histories of quality control and safety. Discard oils that smell or taste bad.

Mold in food is a major cause of food-related illness. Exposure to mold also increases the risk of cancer in both people and pets. Throw away moldy or rancid food in a trashcan that your pet cannot access.

> Just being obese increases your pet's risk of cancer by 15%. "Over-nutrition" and ingestion of too many processed carbohydrates cause more disease in America than malnutrition or deficiency.

☐ **Supplements:** Use supplements wisely and judiciously. Medical mushrooms can stimulate and support immunity. Green tea is preventative and may be useful as an adjunctive therapy in people with cancer. Some supplements for animals contain green tea, but we don't know if this effect crosses over from people to pets at this time. In any case, proper diet is one of the most powerful cancer avoidance choices we can make. Using balanced supplement programs that are not excessive and contain gland extracts, beneficial bacterial strains called probiotics, and digestive enzymes are helpful in some cases, but not all. Many geriatric patients need some additional antioxidant protection. Too many supplements can be harmful and even stress your pet's system, so in many cases use of whole food supplements may be advisable. A knowledgeable integrative veterinarian can help you with these choices.

❑ **Obesity:** Too much nutrition is a bad thing and leads to deposition of materials that the body simply doesn't need. "Over-nutrition" and carbohydrate excess from too many processed carbohydrates cause more disease in America than malnutrition or deficiency. Heart disease, diabetes, arthritis, and stroke are all common diseases that are worsened or predisposed to by obesity. Obesity is strongly related to cancer risks. Just being obese increases your pet's risk of cancer by 15 percent. It causes a 20 percent increase in cancer risk for women related to breast cancer and a 14 percent increase in men related to prostate and other forms of cancer. Some obesity is caused by medical conditions, but most obese pets simply receive too many calories and develop weight issues. They don't need diet pills and appetite suppressants. They need proper amounts of well-balanced nutritious food that is free of excessive loads of chemical agents.

Obesity also robs your pet of energy. Every pound of excess fat leads our bodies to grow one mile of blood vessels. That means a pet's heart, beating 100 times per minute, is forced to pump blood an extra 100 miles each minute for each pound of fat the pet carries. Obesity and inactivity also decrease the activity of your pet's stem cells, which means inactive, overweight pets are less able to repair and rejuvenate their bodies.

That means that if your pet is five pounds overweight, it must expend energy to pump blood an additional 500 miles every minute! That works out to an additional 262,800,000 miles per year. No wonder obese human patients have a higher risk of heart disease!

Keeping pets thin has been shown to increase their life spans by approximately one year (that is seven "human" years). This is a powerful scientific fact. Keep your pet fit and lean if you want it to live longer and healthier. You can conduct a very simple test to determine your pet's body condition. You should be able to feel under its elbow and easily notice its ribs. If there is anything between the skin and ribs in that area, you likely need to help your pet lose weight. Of course it is easier to keep it fit and lean than it is to reduce its weight, so work with your veterinarian and family to keep your pet lean.

❑ **Sleep:** Your pet's body repairs itself during sleep, so be sure that it can get deep, restful, relaxed sleep each day. Sleeping in total darkness increases and normalizes brain production of melatonin and is thought to decrease the risk of several cancers. Sleeping seven hours per night does too. Remove electronics from the sleeping area. LEDs (little lights on power functions and cell phones) flash hundreds of times per second and actually stimulate a part of the brain that decreases melatonin, which can create nervous system stress and decrease the body's ability to properly repair itself. (Some people and pets are more susceptible to this effect than others.)

❑ **Chemicals:** As we discussed earlier, chemicals can damage your pet's terrain and increase its need for certain nutritional items. Chemical exposures can actually lead to malnutrition and a need for excess supplements. Research also has shown that many cancers are related to chemical exposure. Chemicals can enter the body and negatively affect the ability of the immune system. Many chemicals damage or inhibit enzymes needed to create or maintain health. Avoid cheap scented materials, industrial deodorizers, and disinfectants. Pine oil cleaners contain compounds that sensitize pets and damage their nervous systems. Many chemicals can combine and interact, leading to damaged defenses, so reducing chemical exposure is a wise choice. Use proper ventilation when doing construction—wood preservatives, paint and varnish fumes, paint thinners, and other chemicals can lead to physiological damage.

Be aware of the condition of natural bodies of water if your pet swims. Large amounts of toxins can be absorbed through the skin while swimming or bathing. Swimming in water contaminated with chemicals, bacteria, or toxic algae can make your pet sick. If you suspect exposure to toxic or contaminated water, quickly wash your pet with copious clean water from a safe source. Be sure your pet's drinking water is safe. Using a simple water filter on your home tap can do much for your pet's state of health.

Avoid antibiotics except when absolutely needed. Antibiotics do nothing for viral infections, so their routine use for colds and flu makes no medical sense and may increase risks for cancer by damaging healthy mucous membranes in the intestine, killing good bacteria that protect against cancer, and directly damaging the cell's ability to create energy. Eighty percent of the immune system resides around the intestinal system, so anything that damages the integrity of the gut leads to altered immune system function. New research shows that the intestinal system does not return to normal for several weeks to months after antibiotic treatment. Ask your doctor to make recommendations for returning your pet's gut to health after a course of antibiotics is used.

Use prescription drugs only when needed and try to find safer non-drug methods of health care whenever possible. Avoid unnecessary or redundant vaccinations and injections of drugs. In cats, cancer risks are linked to any injection of material as well as vaccines. This fact is known in conventional medicine, and some vaccines are recommended to be given on the leg so if these cancers appear, it is possible to amputate the leg. We must support better vaccine research in the hopes of decreasing this risk. Drug companies and veterinary researchers are working hard to improve this situation.

❑ Avoid chemical dry cleaning, which is strongly linked to increased cancer risk, and don't let your pet sleep in the closet where dry cleaned clothing is stored. Fumes from these dry cleaned clothes may concentrate in the closet. Use wet cleaning or liquid CO_2 cleaning, because these are safer. Avoid contact with preserved wood play sets because their levels of arsenic can cause toxicity and the chemicals used for preservation may be linked to increased cancer risks. Use stainless steel cookware and avoid nonstick cookware (or at least damaged nonstick cookware) to reduce exposure to perfluorooctanoic acid (PFOA), a chemical that is listed by the FDA as a likely carcinogen.

❑ **Emotions:** Life is made up of emotional ups and downs. Having no emotions is not healthy, but avoid long periods of grief and negative emotions, because they sap the immune system of energy and wellness. Some pets are very sensitive to negative emotions. They want you to be happy too, and when you aren't, this can create stress. Have a positive view of Life and take steps to make things work positively so your home is a happier and healthier place for all.

❑ **Probiotics:** Give your pet occasional probiotics because these healthy bacteria stimulate and support bowel health and immune function. Feeding fresh raw greens that have been lightly washed also helps improve the bowel through presence of naturally occurring soil-borne homeostatic bowel organisms. These are powerful assistance for digestion and immunity.

❑ **Detoxification:** Consider routine detoxification thera-py. Proper use of homeopathic, herbal, and nutritional agents actually helps cleanse various body tissues. It is simple to practice spring and fall seasonal cleans-ings. Dogs and cats rarely develop colon toxicity, so harsh laxatives and purgatives are not indicated in dogs and cats. A good integrative or holistic veteri-narian can help choose the strategy that is best for your particular pet.

❑ **Spay/Neuter:** Spaying and neutering decrease the risk of several cancers. Breast cancer is avoidable if pets are spayed before six months of age. Breast cancer risks also drop in pets that are bred more frequently. Certain cancers may increase in dogs that are spayed or neutered (principally cancer of the spleen and bone). However, breast cancer is the number three fatal cancer of dogs, so it is a more common risk than spleen or bone cancer. That said, some dogs have an increased risk for spleen or bone cancer (typically these are more common in large breed dogs), which is a consideration. An option to neutering is vasectomy, however, prostatic problems and behavioral problems are more commonly seen in vasectomized dogs. In cats the strong urine odor and territorial behavior of intact males makes vasec-tomy undesirable.

❑ **Relationships:** Avoid people in personal and profes-sional relationships who are "death talkers" or fear mongers. Some people make their living by scaring others. In some strange way they believe that if people are sufficiently afraid, they will be easier to control. Sometimes this control relates to selling more of a certain product (drugs, vaccines, insurance, etc.). Sometimes it has to do with controlling behavior, as in political manipulations. In any case, stirring up fear involves taking a person from a causal viewpoint and attempting to make her an unwilling effect of something. Regardless of the purpose, if you find someone creating fear without offering a positive action, consider disconnecting from that relationship, especially if the "solution" he offers to the "problem" isn't actually effective. Chronic fear and worry damage living systems. We are not constructed to live in that state. Make health care choices from an informed, positive, causative viewpoint.

❑ **Know Your Pet:** Regularly pet and massage your furry buddy's body. If you notice any bumps or lumps or irregularities, see your veterinarian at once and be sure that fine needle aspirate cytology is performed to screen for cancer. If cancer is found or suspected, deal aggressively with the disease by getting the appropriate tests, surgery, and other supportive means as soon as possible. Find a veterinarian who is knowledgeable about both conventional and holistic cancer therapies.

❑ **Cancer Diagnosis:** If your pet develops cancer:
A. Realize that cancer is biologically a state of confusion, which generalizes into a mental confusion for all involved. Decide to learn about this condition and do your best to help reduce that confusion so you can focus and direct your actions. Take a breath, say a prayer for guidance, and then proceed.

American Veterinary Medical Association's 10 Warning Signs of Cancer in Small Animals

1. Abnormal swellings that persist or continue to grow.
2. Sores that do not heal.
3. Weight loss.
4. Loss of appetite.
5. Bleeding or discharge from any body opening.
6. Offensive odor.
7. Difficulty eating or swallowing.
8. Hesitation to exercise or loss of stamina.
9. Persistent lameness or stiffness.
10. Difficulty breathing, urinating, or defecating.

B. Immediately begin the education process. Seek many different opinions before deciding how to proceed.

C. Realize that feeling confused is part of the condition. As you gain more information you will notice that this confusion decreases until you reach a point of understanding; at that point you are in better shape to make decisions.

D. Use your mind and your innate ability to recognize Truth (intuition) and put fear behind you. Realize that not all cancer is curable but that you can do much to affect your pet's quality of life, and that is important to the outcome.

❑ **Fear:** Don't live your life in fear of cancer or any other thing. Fear is a powerful emotion that directly leads to damage of the immune system. Scientific tests show that fear actually lowers intelligence and problem-solving abilities, so don't stay there for long. Chronic fear exhausts the adrenal gland and compromises the gastrointestinal and respiratory systems. It even changes the state of your nervous system and hormonal functions. Your pet witnesses your fear and if your fear is chronic it can create an unsafe environment. Fear exhausts your pet's psychoneuroendocrine system, which may increase cancer risks, so try to minimize that by becoming informed and taking effective steps. Learning about how to create better quality of life and staying proactive and happy about our connections in life helps us decrease cancer and its harmful effects.

I was once told that the Chinese call cancer "the fear we give others." That means we can decrease cancer by letting go of fear and creating more positive emotions by how we handle our lives. One way to address fear is to replace that feeling with knowledge about the situation. Look, learn, and seek successful outcomes for your pet's problem.

❑ **Health:** Creating health rather than fighting disease is a much superior way to live our lives. In doing so we create ever increasing spheres of health in the world.

> *Cancer is the end of a long process in declining health. Much of this occurs below our level of awareness. Preventing cancer is far more productive than fighting it. Become active in creating health as soon as possible.*

❈ ❈ ❈

Chapter 13. Creating Health Is the Goal

Obtaining and Maintaining Health

Good medicine consists of doing what is needed when it is needed. The funny thing is that most cases I see respond to a very simple, basic program. While simple in its concept, the components of the program must be individualized for each patient's particular lifestyles, environment, and genetic makeup. Developing customized, personalized health programs can be quite involved, but if we keep our minds on this basic road map, we often find health emerging in the most wonderful ways.

Here is the simple plan for recovery or health maintenance:

1. Good stuff in.
We now recognize that most illnesses start with nutritional imbalances, so getting healthy and getting well start by putting real food and healthy nutrients into the body. Good health also consists of putting good thoughts into our world and acknowledging the possibility and desirability of healing in our lives. Good thoughts, good food, good friends, and good works are the basic shopping list needed to create better health.

2. Bad stuff out.

We need to remove toxic foods, bad air, poisoned water, bad energy and thoughts, and destructive behaviors from our lives and those of our pets. This also means allowing the body to conduct its natural detoxification and drainage functions. Therefore, it is good to have inflammation or to discharge materials. Mucus discharge from eyes, mild soft stools, mild coughs, slight redness or itching, and a host of other symptoms relate to this natural detoxification process and should be welcomed. Some pets have more "exciting" signs and these should always be reported to your veterinarian. The bad stuff needs to leave the body for healing to occur, though. When this is happening remember that you asked your pet to get well and this is a necessary part of that process.

3. Monitor the consequences of your actions and inactions over time.

Healing occurs in waves as the body focuses on an area, orders repairs, tears down old structures, and builds new ones. Following that process, the natural healing cycles will repeat. How this occurs is different in every patient depending upon its genetics and resources. We must closely monitor its progress and respond to its specific needs. That may mean being examined at regular intervals by your veterinarian and receiving needed tests such as muscle response, blood, urine, blood pressure, or others that assist your doctor in selecting the best therapy. Everything we do results in some "consequence." The word means "with timing." So eating food may improve signs or worsen them. Supplements may make some things better and cause other signs to appear. Note these carefully and notify your doctor as needed during the entire course of therapy. Realize that change occurs over time so noting your pet's condition and then comparing it to earlier periods is an important part of evaluating its response to the current program.

4.   Communicate honestly with everyone involved. Communication is the hallmark of real healing. Truthful communication is needed to obtain the best results. It is normal to make mistakes; just be sure to tell your doctor so he or she has accurate information when considering your pet's progress and needs. Communication also is involved with your pet's therapy. Acupuncture and body massage actually are means of communicating and developing better health. These methods go far in inducing and enhancing health in our pets. Speak happily and positively. Encourage your pet as well as your veterinarian. Make a safe space for recovery to occur through your handling of communication and you will be rewarded with better, faster results.

What is "good" and "bad" are relative to your specific health needs at any given time. Sometimes it's not so simple to determine if something is good or bad. As an example, if a patient needs antibiotics to survive a life-threatening infection, then antibiotics are "good." If antibiotics are given when they are not needed, they can cause bacterial resistance, nausea, vomiting, diarrhea, lethargy, skin rashes, blood problems, and even injury to microscopic parts of the cell responsible for creating energy. Antibiotics also damage the normal, necessary bacteria called "microflora" which are needed to preserve the health of the gut and immune system. This in turn can cause some pets to become allergic to foods and pollens. If a pet didn't need the antibiotic then its incorrect use as a therapeutic agent is definitely "bad."

The same is true of all drugs and healing medicines☐ when they are needed they are good and when they are not they aren't good. Good communication (speaking, listening, and observing) helps us determine your pet's needs and the results of our actions tell us if we were correct in our assessments or if we need to re-evaluate our conclusions and decisions. Natural health care is very much a team effort. Winning teams communicate regularly and truthfully and they get better results when they do.

Case Reports

The following cases are presented to illustrate particular points. They are not detailed medical case studies designed to teach precisely how to treat each kind of case–that sort of material is not really what this book is about. If you are interested in detailed case reports, I have published many of these in professional journals and they can be found and read at your leisure. These case reports demonstrate that the techniques discussed in this book can help your pet. Realize that every case is different and what works as a miracle for one case will likely not help all other similar-appearing cases. It is so important that everyone understand this fact. Each case is different and needs to be addressed that way for the best results.

The following are examples of what can be achieved by properly aligning the body's natural healing energies with proper nutrition and integrative veterinary medicine.

Allergic Skin Disease, Seizures, Pancreatitis, and Incontinence

Bella is a miracle dog. She has survived well past all her littermates and has had a challenging medical life.

When Bella first came to our office she was suffering from chronic allergic dermatitis, seizures, and chronic pancreatitis. She had no energy and did not feel very playful at all. Any changes in diet or drug therapy could aggravate her pancreatic inflammation and bring on vomiting and nausea. This is not the kind of case we like to have because even simple therapy can trigger serious illness. To make matters worse, her owner was skeptical of holistic medicine and had come to see us at the suggestion of a friend.

Bella's human guardian was a wonderful woman who loved her as a human mother would love her child. Bella had the best of everything but nothing seemed to help her skin. Upon evaluating her we decided to start very slowly. Because Bella's "mom" didn't really feel comfortable with our holistic philosophy, and was concerned about overly severe detoxification symptoms, we started Bella on two simple homotoxicology products. The first medicine, Hepeel, assists the liver in draining toxins and strengthens the intestinal system. The second medicine, BHI Enzyme, supports the energy production mechanisms of the body. We need energy to heal and this is a good way to begin that process.

Bella made immediate improvements. She actually began itching a bit more at first but rapidly calmed down. She had several patches of pigmented skin on her abdomen and her itching became more severe as these pigmented areas became inflamed and cleared toxins. This process took some time but eventually all the excess pigmentation regressed. Over several months she simply resolved her skin problems. Her seizures ceased as well, much to her guardian's pleasure. This was not a surprise to me because Chinese medicine associates disease in the liver with seizures; this is why we started by strengthening Bella's liver.

A year later we received the letter below:

December 17, 2006

Dear Dr. Palmquist,

Thank you for all you did this year to help my ten-year-old pug Bella feel better. Not only did you stop her seizures but you helped alleviate the effects of her pancreatitis as well. Now her bad tummy days when she refuses to eat are rare. And her frequent poo poo accidents, despite four walks a day, are now infrequent. It is such a relief to be able to leave for work and not spend the day worrying about her health. Even better, Bella is back to her perky and playful self. I'll admit I was skeptical in the beginning about your holistic philosophy, but seeing the dramatic results has made me an enthusiastic believer.

Thanks again for helping my precious puggy.

Sincerely,
Staci

Now that is a letter to write home about. Addressing one area led to massive changes for this dog. She began detoxing immediately and did so for several years. Eventually she developed a severe pancreatic inflammation that required hospitalization and extended intensive care, but she made a good recovery and is alive and still receiving regular conventional care as well as acupuncture.

Neuroauricular Therapy with Essential Oils

Hello,

Jess is a twelve-and-a-half-year-old Australian cattle dog who has Cushing's disease. Jess was attacked by a neighbor's dog in November 2007, which marked the beginning of several health issues including a slipped disc, a corneal ulcer, and finally Cushing's. When we first met Dr Palmquist, Jess was very weak and was having difficulty walking. Now, only a month later, Jess is playing happily in the garden. I am delighted with the progress made so far!

Many, many thanks,

Gemma Lawson
June 21, 2009

Veterinarian's Note: This dog had been in pain for months with no relief from standard veterinary care. Gemma did not want surgery and kept seeking a more gentle, natural, and nonsurgical solution. She arrived in our office just after I returned from Ecuador where I learned this technique from human physician Gary Young, ND. Jess was so painful that she would not allow any contact (energetic or physical). She hid under the chair her mom was sitting in, unable to move her head up without terrible pain. After saying a quick prayer for assistance I realized that perhaps I could approach her with essential oils instead. I put some frankincense oil on her head and then found an active scar from an earlier dog attack on her left shoulder area. I put lavender oil on the active scar and it cooled in moments. Fearful at first, she agreed to receive the frankincense oil again, and then returned under the chair to hide. After a few minutes, she felt better and came out to happily accept the neuroauricular therapy procedure using Valor and Deep Relief Young Living Oils. In less than ten minutes she gently raised her head up and looked around, suddenly realizing her pain was gone. Her owner and I cried at that moment and then we laughed a week later when she continued to do well. This was amazing to us all.

Chronic Foot Infection

Zoey was a playful Corgi-mixed-breed dog with a history of severe liver inflammation, which we had brought under control with nutritional therapy and homotoxicology. She had suffered several life-threatening events in her eleven years but always managed to bounce back. After she moved from Los Angeles to Big Bear, California, she developed a severe infection in her toenails. Her local veterinarian did an excellent job of properly working up her case, but to no avail.

Zoey's toes became swollen and red, and literally began to fall off. Because Zoey failed to respond to proper veterinary care, her human mom brought her back to Los Angeles for Nutrition Response Testing℠, which indicated active reflexes for viral and bacterial immune challenges and positive reflexes indicating toxicity from chemicals. Zoey tested weak on liver and pancreatic locations, but these strengthened when we created a program (containing material to support her intestine, liver, spleen, and pancreas) to address an immune challenge to her liver. She was kept on antibiotics in accordance with the laboratory findings and she was prescribed five nutritional whole food supplements. She was also given two homeopathic combination products to activate her immune response to viruses.

When Zoey was rechecked in our office two weeks later, her guardian reported that her condition was cycling between feeling better and being tired. I advised her that this was good and indicated that change was occurring. We retested her with Nutrition Response Testing℠, which now showed active reflexes on the thymus (an important immune organ). When I find animals testing for thymus weakness, this generally indicates a more chronic and deep problem with the immune system. In nearly all these cases we find a positive viral reflex and usually we locate some chemical toxicities as well. Zoey's thymic reflexes normalized when we addressed parasites, viruses, and bacteria. Muscle testing suggested that we change antibiotics and so we did along with adjusting her supplement program to address parasites.

Zoey continued this program until her feet began to heal. This was interesting because she had been on this antibiotic before with no results, so evidently we strengthened her immune system sufficiently for the antibiotic and her immune system to clear her body of illness. She is well maintained now on an integrative program of whole food nutrition and antihomotoxic medication. The whole process took about ninety days, which is typical of such cases. Because the body heals naturally in phases, we usually don't see instant healing but rather several stages of healing as the body addresses different issues in the various organs until it is strong enough to maintain itself again.

Behavioral (Liver/Brain Disease and Obsessive-Compulsive Behavior)

Skittles, a mixed breed dog, was twelve years old when her guardian called me to discuss several health issues. She had recently been vomiting more frequently and was obsessively licking things. Skittles licked sheets and covers as well as her feet when retiring for bed at night. She also licked the floor for hours. The constant licking noise was distracting and kept her guardian from sleeping well.

I knew both the dog and her guardian well and knew that earlier in Skittles' life she had been very sick with a severe form of liver disease. After aggressive conventional and integrative care she had made a full recovery and was doing great. Skittles had previously suffered from seizures, but these hadn't been a problem since her liver had been treated. Nevertheless, this was an important part of her history because it suggested weakness in her neurological system. Regular blood tests supported her recovery from liver disease, but since liver disease can return, I recommended a full examination and blood work-up to see if there were new developments such as anemia or hormonal imbalances.

A few days later we examined Skittles and found her to be doing very well. Her body weight was stable; this was important because sudden weight gain or loss can be a major warning for other diseases such as hormonal imbalances, organ failure, and even cancer. A detailed physical and neurological examination failed to show anything out of the ordinary. We did a full blood panel to evaluate

Skittles' organ functioning and assure that her liver and thyroid were functioning properly and that she was not anemic. The blood work was normal, so we performed some muscle testing and found evidence on Nutrition Response Testing℠ of stressors in the brain and lung. Her liver tested well and this alleviated many of our fears about returning liver disease. Fortunately, a very simple nutritional program seemed to reverse the stressors on Skittles' brain and lungs, so we agreed to try this before reaching for more suppressive and toxic medications.

Skittles' program included a hormone-free extract of neurological tissue and whole food nutrients that support nerve function. Skittles' usual nutritional program included support for her liver and we continued to give this nutrient and glandular support. Her Nutrition Response Testing℠ indicated that additional liver support strengthened the brain so we included that as well, even though it was designed for cats. We instructed that she be given her nutritional program and have her liver rechecked in two weeks. At that time she was taking her supplements well and doing fine. Her liver test was normal. She had ceased vomiting and gained back weight that had been lost. The muscle response testing indicated that her digestion was a bit weak and we found that digestive enzymes strengthened the reflex. These signs indicated a good response, so we continued the program with the addition of some digestive enzymes.

Skittles returned for re-evaluation in six weeks. One vomiting incident had occurred in the last month, which was a great reduction in her normal vomiting frequency. Her guardian reported that she had ceased to lick things and was more active. She was doing incredibly well, a fact that made us all smile. During this consultation I learned that Skittles had regularly suffered from bouts of sleep disturbances, which the owner described as "nightmares." She would cry and run, a behavior that is consistent with altered dream activity. These had ceased since she began her supplemental program, a coincidental occurrence as the compulsive licking stopped.

The last part of this exam was the best. Skittles always hates to see me and other strangers, but on this day we noted that she was wagging her tail and acting especially happy. I learned that she no longer growled and attacked other people and that she was fast becoming everyone's best friend on her walking circuit. I cautiously bent over and she reached out and kissed me on the nose.

"Wow," I thought, "This is the best news of the day."

In Chinese medicine there is a link between liver disease, brain disease, seizures, and aggressive/angry behaviors. In this case it appears that upon finding the right nutritional program we were able to help both organs function better and because of this we could avoid toxic, suppressive drugs that might have been recommended to address a psychiatric disorder called "obsessive-compulsive disorder" or OCD. Those drugs might have worsened her liver condition. In Skittles' case the conventional lab tests were normal and muscle testing found a weakness in the brain and liver. When these were precisely addressed nutritionally the long-term condition simply vanished. That was exciting to see and it makes one a believer in integrative medicine as well.

Nutrition Excess and Supplement Toxicity

When I first saw Neil, I was impressed with how overweight this eight-year-old Collie had become. His owner sought help with chronic diarrhea problems of many years' duration. While taking Neil's history at this visit, I was struck immediately by the dog's diet. His owner was incredibly devoted and she fed the dog only the richest and most expensive, premium diets. These foods were very high in fat and protein and Neil was a pretty quiet older Collie with a weight problem. Other than his weight issues and a bit of arthritis, Neil was pretty healthy, but he suffered from frequent bouts of straining to pass stool, which was often very mucousy and sometimes contained red blood flecks. Such diarrhea is typical with inflammation of the large intestine, a condition we call colitis.

In addition to feeding a very rich diet, Neil's owner insisted on giving many "holistic" dog treats that mostly consisted of freeze-dried organ meat. She also gave the dog massive amounts of several chemically synthetic vitamins to "prevent" disease. She was certain that these things were needed to keep the dog healthy. After forty-five minutes of trying I gave up my efforts to get a diet change and simply took some tests hoping to find a parasite that could explain the diarrhea. Neil's owner agreed to give fewer supplements but still had this dog on so many vitamins that it is a miracle his system could sustain the load. People need to understand that the body must excrete or store excess vitamins and if they are not needed, such massive amounts of supplements can actually increase the workload of the body. The bowel is a favorite system to excrete such material, so diarrhea is a commonly seen side effect in over-supplemented patients.

Stool tests were negative for parasites. However, such tests can miss parasites so we decided to deworm the dog anyway. The diarrhea kept appearing and disappearing and on each presentation I tried desperately to get a simple food change to a prescription food that is high in fiber and low in fat. Finally the owner agreed and the diarrhea vanished in three days!

Unfortunately, the dog's owner read on the Internet that a dog cannot be healthy on such a diet, so she kept taking Neil off the diet, and each time the colitis would return. Finally, after several months of trial and error, Neil's owner saw the truth and agreed to simply stay on the prescription diet. Neil has done well since.

This case shows that not all dogs need tons of supplements and complex diets. Overnutrition is the leading cause of disease in dogs at this time in the United States, which explains the epidemic of obesity that we are currently addressing in veterinary practices across the country. Neil did not need any drugs or alternative therapies to handle his problem. He simply needed the right diet. Sometimes simpler is better and less is more with regard to health.

Feline Skin Problem

Moony was a ten-year-old cat with a history of chronic, itchy dermatitis. He had been treated with steroids and antibiotics and each time his symptoms would disappear, but later flare up again.

His owner carefully controlled his fleas, and this helped, but Moony continued to develop this problem at varying times of the year. Such cases are suspicious for a common feline dermatitis diagnosed as "miliary dermatitis," a form of dermatitis that is commonly diagnosed in conventional veterinary practice.

In Moony's case, when his brother developed an upper respiratory infection with herpes virus, we prescribed a nutritional support product that contained L-Lysine. This amino acid is known to help keep herpes virus from effectively reproducing. Basically it blocks proper assembly of the virus. Moony did not have the virus but we hoped that medical mushrooms and L-Lysine might strengthen his immune system and keep him from getting sick. We had no idea of the surprise that he had in store for us.

Moony's human mom called me and stated that his dermatitis resolved rapidly after beginning the antiherpes virus product. We found this interesting, because we know that herpes virus can cause dermatitis, but it is not commonly diagnosed. In this case we do not know if the nutritional supplement worked or if this was coincidental. Did the mushroom content increase the immune system in some way, banishing the rash? Or did the L-Lysine block an unknown, subclinical herpes virus infection of the skin? We simply don't know, but this case points out why simply using set protocols will not cure most pets of their illnesses. It is essential to treat the individual problem to gain resolution. And just because a case looks similar does not mean it is the same as in cases of other pets with similar signs.

Scars and Aggressive Behavior

Most medical professionals in the United States do not know that scars can seriously interfere with a body's ability to remain in communication and properly monitor and control its normal functioning. Even small scars can cause major disorders in areas such as muscle tone and organ function. For example, it is not uncommon for a middle-aged woman to develop an underactive thyroid that can be related to her episiotomy scar left over from childbirth. Scars can cause disease to surface in veterinary patients as well.

When I was first introduced to the idea of scar therapy I thought it was totally crazy. I did not understand how scars could store up electrical energy and discharge it randomly, completely confusing the body's regulatory system. In my own case, scars on my head, knees, and shoulder were active and after I properly addressed them several medical issues simply vanished. This made me a believer and I sincerely wish more people knew about this issue.

Scooter had a history of being aggressive. Male Schnauzer dogs can be pretty tough and Scooter led the pack in cranky behavior. He was a rescue dog that was approximately eight years old when he first came to our office. His initial examination and blood work were normal. Testing Scooter's blood was an important step because many aggressive dogs have hormonal or liver problems that need to be addressed. Not so with Scooter, though. His blood work was totally normal. Furthermore, Scooter's owner did not want to see an animal behaviorist because she was very much against the use of behavioral drugs in animals. She had read recent accounts of aggression in humans who were prescribed such drugs and was not willing to use them.

Fortunately, our office had other options and so she elected to try Nutrition Response Testing℠ after a few attempts with homeopathic and flower essences failed to solve the problem. When we began to muscle test Scooter I could not get a strong muscle, a fact that might have meant that we would be unable to use muscle response testing in this patient. However, after eliminating many potential causes of the weakness, such as immune challenges, chemical toxicities, metal poisoning, and various dietary allergies and intolerances, I realized that he might have a scar.

The scar from neutering sits right on the midline on an important acupuncture energy channel and is often a problem in aggressive pets, so I checked this muscle response test reflex first and found it to be very weak. We applied a low-energy green laser to the area and then found that daily application of high quality wheat germ oil strengthened the reflex. It was interesting to note that during the laser therapy for his scar, Scooter began to relax and actually started to cooperate with the process. He yawned several times, which is a sign we associate with stress coming off the patient. Yawning during energy therapy usually follows successful actions and often precedes positive responses and progress, so we were happy to see this.

We were able to continue muscle response testing Scooter and found his liver and small intestine to be involved in his weakness. After several weeks of nutritional therapy and scar treatment he became gentle enough that we could muscle test him in the office without incident. He also became more comfortable with strangers and slowly improved over a six-month period of time. During this time he never required behavioral pharmaceuticals.

Cancer: Canine Malignant Melanoma

Note: The following is an excerpt from a formal case publication. The article can be obtained from the American Holistic Veterinary Medical Association: Palmquist RE, Broadfoot PJ. 2008. Two clinical case reports of prolonged survival times following the use of homotoxicology and biological therapy in treatment of canine oral malignant melanoma. JAHVMA.

January 20-28, 2004:

Chula, an eight-year-old, spayed female Rottweiler was presented for routine vaccination and wellness evaluation. Rabies vaccination was delayed because her examination revealed a 2-cm pigmented oral mass on the left upper maxillary area. Chest radiographs revealed no visible metastasis and routine blood evaluation was performed. The dog was scheduled for surgery and the mass excised by lumpectomy on the following day. Chula was released on a homeopathic medicine called Traumeel® and an antibiotic for seven days.

A biopsy revealed oral melanosarcoma, an aggressive oral tumor known to spread quickly. A very guarded prognosis was given and due to the aggressive nature of these tumors the dog was referred to an oncologist for discussion of further options, including potential inclusion in a study involving melanoma vaccination protocols.

A needle aspirate of the regional lymph node failed to demonstrate spread of the tumor. The oncologist commented:

> *The longest survival time reported to date in dogs with oral melanoma are those with small tumors (< 2 cm) that are surgically removed and followed by surgery with radiation and chemotherapy. These pets live an average of one year. Without therapy or in the face of metastasis, I believe this number would drop to six months. Other options include chemo or radiation alone or a tumor vaccine.*

The family returned home to await news of their acceptance or rejection for inclusion in the tumor vaccination study.

March 9-11, 2004:

Chula was presented for routine evaluation postoperatively. She had received no other treatments. A large, golf ball-sized mass was now present on the neck in the submandibular lymph node region, which in-house cytology confirmed as spread of the oral tumor to the local lymph node. The oncologist called to advise Chula's owners that she was denied participation in the vaccine study. When Chula could not gain access to the experimental melanoma vaccine experiment, the owners decided against further aggressive therapy (radiation, surgery, and chemotherapy) and requested a biological therapeutic approach. I advised them that such treatment was experimental and had not been evaluated in peer-reviewed journals. They agreed to therapy and the dog was treated by mixing her blood with a series of homeopathic agents, which serve to activate the immune and detoxification systems. We also prescribed a vitamin mixture for nutritional support called TF Canine Complete® and scheduled a recheck appointment for two weeks.

March 25, 2004:

Chula looked bright, vital, and more energetic, and was feeling very well, according to her owners. She had gained three pounds of body weight. The large lymph node in her neck had shrunken and was about 0.5 to 1 cm in diameter. We continued Chula's health care program and added oral sodium ascorbate along with 3V Caps ES (salmon oil). Recheck was recommended for two weeks later.

April 19, 2004:

Chula had been depressed and lost weight for three days. Her appetite was reduced and her owners had stopped her supplements, fearing a reaction. The lymph node in the neck was nearly gone and the owners were advised that this likely represented regression of the tumor, which was desirable. Stronger anticancer homeopathics were given and we decided to watch her carefully.

May 17, 2004:

Chula began limping and appeared disoriented and dizzy. She had vomited twice and had intermittent low-back and hip pain. She also had skin irritation around her vulva. Her owners did not want to take X-rays or other tests. Natural healing is frequently accompanied by discharge of materials as the body eliminates homotoxins. In this case, we suspected she was clearing toxic material through her colon and connective tissues. She was on homeopathics for pain and energy production and a new formula to assist her arthritis pain.

June 16, 2004:

Marked diarrhea suddenly appeared from the large intestine. This was evidence of her body's effort to remove toxins and we were happy to see this. Her arthritic pain had vanished and she was moving better with less stiffness or pain on palpation of the area.

July 15, 2005:

One year had passed and Chula continued to feel well with mild rear leg soreness. The owners declined pain medication because they were concerned that this might block healing. The cervical lymph node was approximately 2 cm in size but stable, according to the owner. Homeopathic and nutritional care were continued.

February 16, 2006:

Chula was doing well. The cervical mass had vanished completely. The mass in the thoracic inlet was stable and palpated as a soft, noncancerous, fatty mass. Vitality was excellent for a dog two years post surgery with metastatic melanoma. Her weight was stable at 82 lbs.

Chula at 1,579 days of survival.

April 3, 2007:

A phone call from the owners reported that Chula had been coughing. Because we feared return of the tumor we recommended chest x-rays. No tumor was evident so a needle aspirate of the neck lymph node was performed, yielding only mature fatty tissue with no cancer evident.

Chula passed away of old age in 2008. At the time of her diagnosis her chances to live more than a year were small. The best guess was that she would live three to six months. She fooled all of us and conquered her disease, living four and a half years. Although we are not as successful with many other forms of cancer, we have now treated several dogs with melanoma and seen similar success stories. Chula's successful life and her dedicated owners opened the door for other dogs with this disease. I will always smile when I think of her.

Hair Loss, Skin Pigmentation, and Food Allergy

Ellie presented to our clinic as a rescue in December 2006. She suffered from skin problems and was on cortisone. Her skin was bald and black. Tests showed no parasites. While she was at the local animal shelter she had been attacked and received appropriate tests for skin parasites and fungal infections, but nothing was found. We placed her on a duck and potato diet and she developed diarrhea so we removed the food.

I gave her some antihomotoxic medicine to support her skin and liver and we sent a full blood test to the lab. In the meantime we began to detox her liver and support her skin nutritionally. She developed diarrhea almost immediately, which suggests food allergy or detoxification. Tests for parasites and abnormal hormone levels were negative, and several diet changes helped, but none resolved the diarrhea. Another veterinarian prescribed antibiotics, which slightly improved her stools, but we knew something was still to blame for her current state. We tried her on a different venison diet and her diarrhea returned.

Two months later Ellie returned and had grown substantial hair, especially in the region around her eyes. She still had diarrhea problems, though. We were ecstatic because in natural healing we know that healing occurs from inside to outside and from the head down. We also know that the body eliminates toxins through the bowel, so it appeared that Ellie was doing exactly what she needed to do to improve her health. We prescribed a homeopathic detoxification program to assist her.

A month later her examination revealed continued slow hair regrowth. We switched her to a duck and potato limited-antigen prescription diet and her soft stool resolved. Her hair continued to slowly grow in for several months, during which time we supported her with various antihomotoxic medicines. Five months after her first examination she began to regrow hair rapidly, so we continued her duck and potato diet and homeopathic medicines.

Ellie's diarrhea returned and was refractory to many different attempts at control. Because her skin was reversing so rapidly we continued to work with her diarrhea, but looked at it as a blessing that meant she was clearing toxic material from her system. Three months later she developed a bad cough that worsened at night. This was treated with antihomotoxic agents that support the immune system against viruses. She also received antibiotics for her condition and she recovered nicely.

Three months after this Ellie began itching severely and her owner elected to use drugs to control the itching. Two months later we were able to stop the drugs and she continued to slowly improve. More than a year later Ellie developed pain over her gallbladder area, which I treated with a homeopathic for the liver. She responded well. Four months after that she suffered a series of seizures and went back on steroids for her skin. This followed eating some duck jerky treats. We instructed her owner to cease the treats and stay just on the duck and potato diet and she improved. Her blood test revealed some liver inflammation and she was placed on nutritional supplements for her liver. As her liver cleansed itself her skin healed further and now she is maintained on just the duck and potato diet.

Every time we see Ellie we all smile and are grateful for her mom's patience in allowing her to remove those toxins and slowly repair her body.

A Double Whammy: Parvovirus and Canine Distemper Virus

Many people have never seen a case of canine distemper, thanks to the effectiveness of modern vaccinations; however, this viral disease of dogs is a devastating condition. The distemper virus of dogs is in the measles virus family; once infected, it rapidly spreads to nearly all tissues in the body. It enters through the respiratory lining and causes a mild upper respiratory condition that resembles a cold. After several days this seems to resolve, but actually the virus goes deeper into the body and then returns after about two weeks in a terrible form involving the lungs and often the brain. Pneumonia and seizures occur. Most cases are seen in younger, unvaccinated dogs, but a devastating form called "old dog encephalitis" occurs in older dogs.

In unvaccinated dogs, these processes proceed so rapidly that the puppy may be overwhelmed and die or require euthanasia. When I went to veterinary school we were taught that there was nothing to be done for these dogs and that euthanasia was an appropriate treatment, especially once they reached the brain infection phase. Recovering dogs often have neurological disability, visual problems from retinal injury, and seizures. Because the virus infects all epithelial tissues in the body, distemper survivors can show disease in any system of the body (runny nose, sinusitis, pneumonia, gastrointestinal upsets, urinary infections, skin problems, and neurological complications such as tics and grand mal seizures). Such conditions can last a lifetime, and some may resolve over time.

Our practice is located in an area of Los Angeles that sees many canine distemper cases. Unvaccinated dogs roam the streets and spread this deadly virus. It's sad too, because simply vaccinating dogs once or twice is highly effective in preventing this crippling disease. In nearly thirty years of practice, I've never seen a case of full-blown canine distemper in a properly vaccinated dog. Our practice has had a unique opportunity to see more canine distemper than most practices and we have cooperated with amazing animal stewards and saved many dogs from this terrible condition. My office manager and technician both own dogs that survived distemper and are now normal.

My first success in treating canine distemper involved a lovely puppy named Rocky. Rocky was unlucky enough to catch another deadly disease called canine parvovirus. He presented to our office in shock with severe diarrhea. Parvovirus strips the intestines of their protective lining and attacks the dog's immune system directly. It may also infect and damage puppies' hearts. Severe vomiting and diarrhea coupled with immune collapse makes these dogs prone to systemic bacterial infection caused by their own natural bacteria. Death is common without treatment.

While Rocky was undergoing intensive care for his parvovirus, he developed additional symptoms of canine distemper—a particular nasty symptom we call chewing gum seizures. These progressed to generalized seizures as the virus damaged his brain's neural tissue. I called Rocky's owner to recommend euthanasia because this was viewed as the compassionate way to proceed at that time. Rocky's owner was the best friend of my animal health technician and had been referred to our office because of that friendship, and a promise of my effectiveness in Rocky's care. This was a particularly uncomfortable and sad moment for me, as I admitted that I was unable to do more for this cute little dog.

Rocky's owner considered the facts and told me that she knew I could help him and that I should do all I could. I repeated the grave prognosis and the expense involved, but she was firm in her resolve. I hung up the phone and had no idea what I would do, but began to treat Rocky with massive levels of vitamins A, B, and C, along with intensive intravenous fluids and antibiotics to keep him better hydrated and control his secondary infections. For three long days, Rocky suffered off and on from seizures and was a shuddering mass of quivering flesh. We used conventional drugs to partially control his grand mal seizures. Both diseases wracked his tiny body.

Suddenly he began to improve, but his neurological problems continued. We continued to support him but didn't expect much of an outcome. Much to my surprise, then, Rocky rallied and was able to go home. After several weeks he developed a terribly itchy skin problem that is characteristic of canine distemper virus in the skin. He also developed detoxification symptoms as the virus was purged from his urinary system. In each case we supported him with agents that help the immune system and fed his tissues as they attempted the monumental effort toward repair.

After two long years he made a complete recovery, and it was so joyful seeing him for an annual physical exam instead of a medical visit. Rocky had suffered from recurring allergies before his battle with distemper, and these vanished and he leads a normal, happy life much to the joy of his owner, my technician, and me.

We pursued Rocky's treatment because his human mom loved him so much and because she refused to accept conventional wisdom. Now, a decade later, we openly discuss treating canine distemper with our clients. Rocky's story opened the door for many other dogs to get a second chance. We now use a balanced combination of homeopathy and nutritional and herbal therapies to address this disease in dogs. We smile each time we see one of our survivors.

Rocky's story is an example of how science and medicine are supposed to interact. We use proven treatments when we can, but when the books and experts say that there is no hope, we use intellect and love to attempt to find new treatments. Then, when we succeed, we tell others. In this way more knowledge builds and fewer pets die needlessly.

For an interesting documentary about another case of canine distemper from our practice, visit http://www. youtube.com/watch?v=Q1z9KIMLt6k. This is the story of puppy named Jack. He was rescued from the streets of Los Angeles by a loving couple and battled severe distemper for more than a year before eventually making a full recovery. It's a heartwarming story that emphasizes the power of cooperation, patience, persistence, and love in healing.

Not all dogs with canine distemper can be saved, and many may be neurologically crippled for long periods of time. Some permanently disabled dogs have seizures or tics or are blinded by the disease. Treatment takes many months and is terribly hard and emotionally draining for all involved. This is why it is so critical that dogs be properly vaccinated for distemper. Only a few shots must be given to puppies to effectively prevent the disease for a lifetime. Repeated booster vaccinations are usually unnecessary, and we advise that owners simply test their dog's blood annually to make sure that there is adequate protection against distemper virus.

The prudent use of vaccinations to prevent this horrible disease, coupled with the use of conventional medicines and alternative modalities to treat the unfortunate dogs that contract the disease, represents a balanced integrative practice that helps keep us all smiling for long periods of time. As we seek and apply Truth we find healing, even in such difficult conditions as canine distemper.

☆ ☆ ☆

Chapter 14. Closing Comments

I hope this book will help people take a different view of veterinary health care. We live in an age in which technological miracles are possible, but we need to remember that the greatest miracles come from Life itself: A puppy playing. A kitten leaping. A beloved canine friend joining us for a walk or jog. An aged pet resting comfortably at our feet or on our lap. Each of these contains a body that is breathing and processing many different types of energy and information to bring about extended survival. Life is in each of us today, and each body we see represents millions of years of fine tuning.

If we educate ourselves and associate with those who have our best interests in mind, then I believe we can all learn better ways to live. If we learn to communicate more effectively with our bodies and those of our patients, then miracles can certainly happen. If we take these healthier bodies and use them for higher purposes, then the world can witness the birth of a newer, better civilization. I dream of these things daily.

Every day we learn more about health and health care, and each day we implement these philosophies in our practice. As we learn more about how everything functions we can develop new tools to cooperate more effectively with our biological systems. This is an exciting possibility. The future is bright indeed.

My entire staff wishes you success on your journey to happiness and better health. We, and the growing community of integrative and holistic veterinarians, await the opportunity to help you on this trip. We want you to know that no one is alone in this world unless they fail to reach out to others. We are here for you, whenever you need us. If our practice is not the right place for you then seek out other holistically inclined veterinarians at the Web site for the American Holistic Veterinary Medical Association: www. AHVMA.org.

Go well. Do well. Farewell for now.

Love, Light, and Life,
Dr. Palmquist and the Staff of Centinela Animal Hospital
www.LovAPet.com

✭ ✭ ✭

References And Suggested Reading

Richard Palmquist, DVM, Centinela Animal Hospital. 721 Centinela Avenue, Inglewood, CA 90302. (310) 673-1910, www.LovAPet.com. Hours by appointment. We do not do phone consultations.

Web sites

http://www.nutritiondata.com/tools/nutrient-search (Look up nutritional data.)

http://www.balanceit.com (Nutritional Web site for producing a balanced diet under supervision of board certified veterinary nutritionists.)

http://www.susanwynn.com. (Susan Wynn, DVM, past president of the AHVMA and a clinical resident in veterinary nutrition. An excellent nutritional consultant with extensive experience in alternative medicine.)

http://www.unsinc.info/contact.html. (Ulan Nutritional Systems, Inc. Professional site for doctors interested in learning more about Nutrition Response Testing^{sm}.)

http://www.ppnf.org/catalog/ppnf/pottenger.htm. Price-Pottenger Nutrition Foundation. Information of nutrition and unprocessed foods.

Reading Resources

The Nature of Animal Healing: The Definitive Holistic Medicine Guide to Caring for Your Dog and Cat, Martin Goldstein, DVM.

Integrating Complementary Medicine into Veterinary Practice, Robert Goldstein, Paula Jo Broadfoot, Richard Palmquist, Karen Johnston, Jui Jia Wen, Barbara Fourgere, with Margo Roman.

Pottenger's Cats: A Study in Nutrition, Francis Marion Pottenger, Jr., MD.

Whole Food Nutrition: The Missing Link in Vitamin Therapy: The Difference Between Nutrients WITHIN Foods vs. Isolated Vitamins & How They Affect Your Health, Vic Shayne, PhD.

In Defense of Food: An Eater's Manifesto, Michael Pollan.

The Hundred-Year Lie: How to Protect Yourself from the Chemicals That Are Destroying Your Health, Randall Fitzgerald.

The Great Health Heist, Paul Rosen, JD., L.Ac.

Professional Organizations

Courses in continuing education and certification in alternative medicine can be obtained by licensed veterinarians from the following reputable organizations:

American Academy of Veterinary Acupuncture (AAVA)

100 Roscommon Drive, Suite 320
Middletown, CT 06457
(860) 632-9911 8:30 a.m.-6:00 p.m. Eastern Time
AAVA.org

The Academy of Veterinary Homeopathy (AVH)
PO Box 9280
Wilmington, Delaware 19809
(866) 652-1590 (Voice & Fax, US and Canada)
www.theavh.org

American Holistic Veterinary Medical Association (AHVMA)
Carvel Tiekert, DVM, Executive Director
2218 Old Emmorton Road
Bel Air, MD 21015
(410) 569-0795, fax (410) 569-2346
www.ahvma.org

American Veterinary Chiropractic Association (AVCA)
442154 E 140 Rd
Bluejacket, OK 74333
918-784-2231 Fax 918-784-2675
www.animalchiropractic.org

International Veterinary Acupuncture Society (IVAS)
PO Box 271395
Fort Collins, Co 80527
(970) 266-0666
www.ivas.org

Veterinary Botanical Medicine Association (VMBA)
Jasmine C. Lyon, Executive Director
1785 Poplar Dr.
Kennesaw, GA 30144
www.vbma.org

✲ ✲ ✲

Made in the USA
Lexington, KY
23 July 2014